NEW MEXICO
BOOK OF THE
UNDEAD

NEW MEXICO BOOK OF THE UNDEAD

Goblin & Ghoul Folklore

RAY JOHN DE ARAGÓN

Published by The History Press
Charleston, SC 29403
www.historypress.net

Copyright © 2014 by Ray John de Aragón
All rights reserved

First published 2014

Manufactured in the United States

ISBN 978.1.62619.732.9

Library of Congress CIP data applied for.

Notice: The information in this book is true and complete to the best of our knowledge. It is offered without guarantee on the part of the author or The History Press. The author and The History Press disclaim all liability in connection with the use of this book.

All rights reserved. No part of this book may be reproduced or transmitted in any form whatsoever without prior written permission from the publisher except in the case of brief quotations embodied in critical articles and reviews.

*With heartfelt appreciation to Rosa María Calles, a leading folklorist and preserver of Hispanic culture,
and Rosalía de Aragón, an interpreter of New Mexico folklore through her Chautauqua performances.*

This book is dedicated to María Cleofas Sanchez de Aragón, Aurora Lucero, Cleofas Jaramillo, Fabiola Cabeza de Baca, Juan B. Rael and all those who were committed to passing on our Spanish folkloric tradition to others as oral storytellers. When the Spanish colonists arrived in New Mexico in 1598, they brought centuries-old stories of enchanted castles, princesses and evil or warm-hearted kings and queens along with them. Spanish women in the colony preserved or developed their own stories of monsters, ghosts and witches to keep their children in check and for them to take care of themselves. Many stories were meant to entertain listeners, but they were also moralizing and maintained the principles of right and wrong. The teaching of and making good decisions was the intention of fables, legends, myths and proverbs. Hopefully this very rich and vibrant heritage will be continued for future generations through these tales.

Contents

After World	9
Introduction: Tales That Never Die	11

Part I. Goblins and Ghouls

Historical Overview	19
Night Walker—Thunder Mountain Goblin	25
La Guajona—Vampire Witch	33
La Llorona—Wailing Woman	41
Lobisón—Attack of the Werewolf	51

Part II. The Undead

Historical Overview	61
Santa Companía—Holy Company	69
Dead Ringer	75
Bibiana	85
María Sangre Fría—Bloody Mary	91
Knock, Knock, Who's There?	99
In the Gloom of the Night	107
La Muerte Pays a Visit	113
About the Author	123

Seventeenth-century vellum prints of mythical creatures. *Courtesy of the author.*

After World

Cuatro Esquinas Tiene Mi Morada

Cuatro esquinas tiene mi morada,
Cuatro ángeles que las adornan,
Miguel, Rafael, Gabriel, y Ángel
Guardián.
Ni brujas ni herejotes
Ni otro malhechor
Podrá entrar aquí.

En el nombre del Padre,
Y del Hijo, y del Espíritu Santo.
Amén.

Abiquiú, Nuevo México, 1763

My Abode Has Four Corners

My abode has four corners,
Four angels that adorn them,
Michael, Raphael, Gabriel, and
Guardian Angel.
Neither witches, nor great heretics
Nor other evildoer
Will ever enter here.

In the name of the Father,
the Son, and the Holy Spirit.
Amen.

Abiquiú, New Mexico, 1763

La Tumba
by *Miguel Martínez y Santistevan*
"El Anciano de Taos"
circa 1895

En estas tristes soledades,
en el profundo silencio,
en estos bosques sombríos,
bajo estos árboles frescos,
sin cuidados ni inquietudes,
libre de remordimientos,
ni envidiado ni envidioso,
feliz mi vida mantengo.

The Tomb

In this sad solitude,
In this profound silence,
In this shady forest,
Under these fresh trees,
Without cares or anxiety,
Free of remorse,
Neither envied nor with envy,
I happily maintain my life.

At the End

Ravens cawing,
Black cats meowing,
Scarecrows waving,
Werewolves searching,
Witches flying,
Storm clouds brewing,
Lightning flashing,
Winds a howling,
Undead walking,
Frightening nightmares,
Spirits crying,
Tombstones waiting.

Introduction
Tales That Never Die

Along the lush green banks of the Río Grande, *la gente*, the people, lived, prayed, cried and laughed. Spirits of the old ones nurtured the rich perfumed earth. *Los Hispanos* understood the joyous meaning of life in the beautiful winding valleys, but they also felt the very forceful presence of Doña Sebastiana, Death. The knowledge of being and passing was learned from *Los Antepasados*, those who came before. This wonderful heritage was passed down through *los dichos*, folk sayings, that mingled harmoniously with the haunting *alabado* chants of the *Penitentes* and the stories of the elders, which flowed onward incessantly like the nurturing water of the river.

The Sangre de Cristo Mountains near Santa Fé in New Mexico convey the aura, mystery and intrigue of the land. The enchanting blue and blood-red skies capture the imagination of residents and visitors alike. An indelible perception of life and death, what is real and what is not and what could be is the attraction that draws everyone. The splendor and awe of places like Taos and iconic sites such as the Santuario de Chimayo and White Sands stand as a testament of the ancient folkways that linger on into the present. No one can escape the nostalgia and the spellbinding sentimentality that is filled with wonderful history and enduring romance. *Viene del corazón*, it comes from the heart. There are beautiful *recuerdos*, memories from the ancestors, and *cuentos*, stories lovingly passed down from one generation to the next.

It is a marvelous setting of natural inspiration. While gazing at the scenic wonders of *Nuevo México*, creative energies flow through the veins of the hills and valleys. Supernatural visions emerge and illuminate the cornucopia of

Introduction

stories that are embedded in the earth of New Mexico. Winds whisper tales that cast a shadow in the night. Spirits continue to roam freely and happily. It is the secret passage into myth and legend.

When the Spanish colonists arrived in 1598, life was hard in this isolated frontier of the Spanish Empire. Hardworking settlers raised sheep and crops and braved floods, drought and ceaseless raids by Indians. Extremes of heat and the deep snows of winter were endured. Spanish tradition was ingrained into the territory. Franciscan friars established a string of mission churches in the outlying Indian pueblos. Along with the churches, they set up schools and guilds to train the natives in the arts. The friars taught the Indians crafts and agricultural techniques that led to new livelihoods. The Franciscans also told Aesopian fables that the Indians learned. Stories of enchantment and *Arabian Nights* tales were also popular.

Los ciboleros, the rough and tough Hispanic New Mexican horsemen who hunted buffalo, bear and deer, characterized New Mexico in the late eighteenth and early nineteenth centuries. The fearless *Comancheros* were also the stuff of legends at this time in that these Spanish horsemen traveled deep into Indian enemy territory to trade with the Comanche Indians. The Comanches respected the nerve and fighting skills of the Comancheros. Stories were often told around Hispanic New Mexican campfires about the valiant Comancheros, and *corridos*, ballad songs, were composed and sung in their honor. It was said they could fight the fiercest grizzly or mountain lion and stare death in the face as well.

The storytelling tradition in early New Mexico took on a variety of forms with theater, music and the ever-popular oral stories that taught lessons. Roman Catholic worship, which Spanish settlers brought to the New World in the seventeenth century, played an important role in the spiritual life of isolated Spanish communities of the Southwest. It is revealed in the historical and artistic roots of the religious faith that inspired them and is at the center of most of the stories that were told and passed on. Among favorite stories were tales of witches and ghosts. These stories might have been derived from actual historical events. Some of these peculiar events led to the naming of locations and towns. Many myths involving owls and their transformation into witches arose and spread throughout New Mexico. Of course, during this time, stories of witches were prevalent everywhere. It's interesting to note that local musicians played their homemade fiddles and guitars and wrote songs dedicated to everything that surrounded them. They sang about the birds, their horses and farm animals. Some of the songs were whimsical, while others showed their love for them. They wrote songs and music for weddings, baptisms and everyday experiences. In the village of El Duende (Goblin Town) near Taos, violinists played folk music from the colonial period. People thoughtfully listened to pieces that dealt with spirits and sadly reminisced when they heard *La Entriega de los Difuntos* ("The Release of the Dead"). They told their stories through music and thus recorded for all time the history of the people.

Gifted storytellers in the Spanish villages and towns of New Mexico were simple farmers, ranchers, sheepherders, wives, mothers and grandmothers. Old World customs were observed. Many stories were told about youths who were helped by supernatural forces and through this succeeded in marrying princesses. Tricksters and greedy people paid for their misdeeds. There are stories about those who feared nothing, not even ghosts. Tales of sorcerers, witchcraft and also saints were narrated and embellished with people's names and the names of communities to make the stories more dramatic and realistic. Variations of the story of *Cenicienta*, Cinderella, and of *La Llorona*, the Wailing Woman, are numerous. Tales of those who were turned into animals through a spell and saved by a hero or heroine were preserved. Women's struggles, violence against women, gender-based bullying, relationships between people, ignorance, stereotypes, understanding of the past and present, anti-bias, parenting and safety are all subjects of New Mexico stories. People learned about caring for the less fortunate and to treat others with respect. A person's word stood for truth and honor. Lifelong skills were learned through stories such as the following, a treatment of the ethereal that can do us harm.

It was a Saturday night in the Medina home. The evening meal had already been served. Dishes had been washed and put away. Leftovers were neatly placed in the icebox, and the final tidying up was done. The children—Filomena, aged nine; Victoria, aged seven; and Roberto, aged six—rushed to the living room and took their places on the floor next to the fireplace. Their parents were Leonor and Juanita. They were already sitting and waiting. Old grandmother Benigna finally walked in and sat in her favorite easy chair. Every Saturday, after a hard week of work, it was time to have fun. It was storytelling time. The children eagerly and impatiently waited. Nana Benigna was ready to tell the story called "Los Ojos de la Bruja," the Eyes of the Witch.

The soft-spoken grandmother was already ninety years old, and she knew many stories. She lived in a small adobe house that was built next to the main house. It was only one large room with a wood-burning stove, a chest for her prized possessions and a little cot. Benigna, which in Spanish means "kind"

Introduction

or "nice," had a place for her clothes and another for her necessities. It was all that she needed. Walking into her little home was like stepping back in time. The old woman walked with a cane and always wore an apron. All of her long dresses had prints of small flowers. She liked her high-laced black shoes and her gold-rimmed glasses. The children spent a great deal of time with their loving grandmother. They helped her feed the chickens and tend to her garden. They also helped with her goose, Pulitó. That goose could be mean. It didn't like strangers. It protected its mistress very well. Benigna was highly respected in the community and very wise. The Medina family was proud of her. Not a single decision of importance was made without her counsel. She was the matriarch of the family, and everyone sought out her advice. Benigna was strong, healthy and happy. She lived a good life. She finally began telling a story.

> *Once there was a couple who became deathly ill. Their names were Ricardo and Máxima. For some reason, Máxima started up with a stomachache one day. It got steadily worse. Then, strangely, Ricardo also got a terrible stomachache. His pains wouldn't go away either. It wasn't a natural illness. It was something else. It was a witch's potion. Not far from where Ricardo and Máxima lived was the home of a woman they called* Ceniza, *ashes. It seems that Ceniza gave the couple a delicious pie. After they ate some, they got sick. Doña Maribela, the local* curandera, *a medicine woman who healed with herbs and roots, was called. She cured the couple, but she suspected that a witch had given them the pie. She immediately left for Ceniza's home.*
>
> *She found her sitting on her rocking chair. There was no way to tell if Ceniza was a witch or not, but Doña Maribela could see it in her eyes. Her eyes were different. They were so bright they almost glowed, even in the daytime. At night, her eyes seemed to have light that came out of them. Doña Maribela knew that if Ceniza did not tell the truth, her eyes would get brighter. When the curandera confronted Ceniza, she of course said it was ridiculous for her to suspect she was a witch. When Doña Maribela asked her a set of questions, Ceniza's eyes got brighter and brighter with each answer. Doña Maribela knew once and for all that Ceniza was a witch. Doña Maribela told the witch that if she ever did anything like that again, she would have to answer to her.*

Nana Benigna then went into other stories that had to do with lying and telling the truth. These were "Juan Verdades," a story about a boy who

Introduction

couldn't lie even if his life depended on it, and "La Hija del Diablo," one about a girl who could never tell the truth. Early New Mexico storytellers were experts at spinning tales of accomplishment through good deeds. Many stories that are found are of Old World origin, beautifully preserved for centuries since the first Spanish settlers introduced them into the area. Tales of local origin deal more with superstition and death. Perhaps this was because life was hard on the frontier. Warring Indians were always a threat, settlements were isolated and the night was especially foreboding. These were the perfect ingredients to nourish superstition.

Everyone knows that it's bad luck to spill salt. Never walk under ladders or let a black cat cross your path. If you accidently break a mirror, this will be followed by seven years of misfortune. In other words, always be very, very careful. Friday the thirteenth brings on many fears, especially when the day is accompanied by a full moon. Buildings do not have a thirteenth floor but simply go from the twelfth to the fourteenth. People stay locked up at home on Friday the thirteenth and will not report to work. The number 666 is supposedly the devil's sign. Phone companies will not use this number as a prefix. It is a number to steer away from. The "Fearsome Six" seldom get together, but when they do, it is catastrophic. These minions of evil are the vampire, the werewolf, the witch, the ghoul, the goblin and death. They are in the shadows, waiting. They are also in these stories. Tales about them never die. A Spanish colonial musical piece that was once played was "El Baile de los Duendes," the Dance of the Goblins. Perhaps the goblins will dance once again.

PART I
GOBLINS AND GHOULS

Historical Overview

A La Ru

A la ru, mi hito,
Duermase ya,
Que viene el coco
Y se lo comerá.
A la ru, a la ru, a la ru.

Rock-a-bye baby,
Go to sleep now,
The boogieman's coming and he will eat you.
Rock-a-bye, rock-a-bye, rock-a-bye.

Children and infants the world over have been put to sleep with gentle and soothing nursery rhymes. The reality is that most nursery rhymes are rooted in superstition and fear. Some origins can be traced to the plagues that ravished Europe. Others developed from times of war, pestilence and storms. Who has not heard of the famous lullaby "Rock-a-Bye Baby"?

Rock-a-bye baby, in the treetops,
When the wind blows, the cradle will rock.
When the bough breaks, the cradle will fall,
And down will come baby, cradle and all.

Le Ghoul from *Ars Moriendi*, block print, unknown printer, 1465. *Courtesy of the author.*

Some of the nursery chants came about during medieval times and were meant to keep evil at bay. Proverbs, sayings or rhymes admonished children to be careful at night: "The day has eyes, and the night has ears," "Tonight upon your pillow, close your eyes and hide your head, for the witches and goblins will be hovering over your bed," "Crisscross, double cross, tells the monster to get lost." Adults were told, "Walk three times backwards around your home before the sun sets to keep evil spirits away."

Werewolves were especially feared. Around the fifteenth century, it was written that "even he who is pure of heart and says his prayers by night, may become a wolf when the wolf bane blooms and the moon is full and bright." People believed that if a person's third finger on each hand was as long or longer than the second finger, then that person was a werewolf. They also thought that if the wolf bane plant with its purple-hooded flowers bloomed and someone was standing nearby, then that person could turn into a werewolf. Werewolves slept with one eye open and their thumbs linked. Their eyebrows met. They cast a hypnotic gaze and drew their strength from the moon. Werewolves had the power to control all creatures of the night. Of course, werewolves were associated primarily with men, not women.

One of the most interesting women from scary European folklore other than *La Llorona*, the Wailing Woman, is Bloody Mary. She is one of the dark specters that plague children. Many oral stories are told about her ghoulish hair-raising haunts. For example, since a mirror is always associated with her ability to appear, she is forever trapped within one. It is not generally known that this spine-tingling legend traces its origins to Mary Queen of Scots. Queen Mary was imprisoned in the black and forbidding Loch Leven Castle. She had a legitimate claim to the throne of England, and Queen Elizabeth I signed her death warrant to remove her as an obstacle. It is said that the hapless queen spent her final tragic hours looking into a mirror as she dressed and groomed her hair. She wanted to look her best for her final day. The executioner had to strike her three times before cutting off her head. They claim that after her horrifying death, her spirit roamed and that people looking into the mirror could see her standing behind them. Through the eerie mirror, Mary could emerge into the natural world if someone holding a lit candle at night and chanting her name three times summoned her. She was there in the mirror, watching you and hoping you would call her. She could even pull you into the mirror, never to be seen again. Bloody Mary dolls were popular for a time during Halloween.

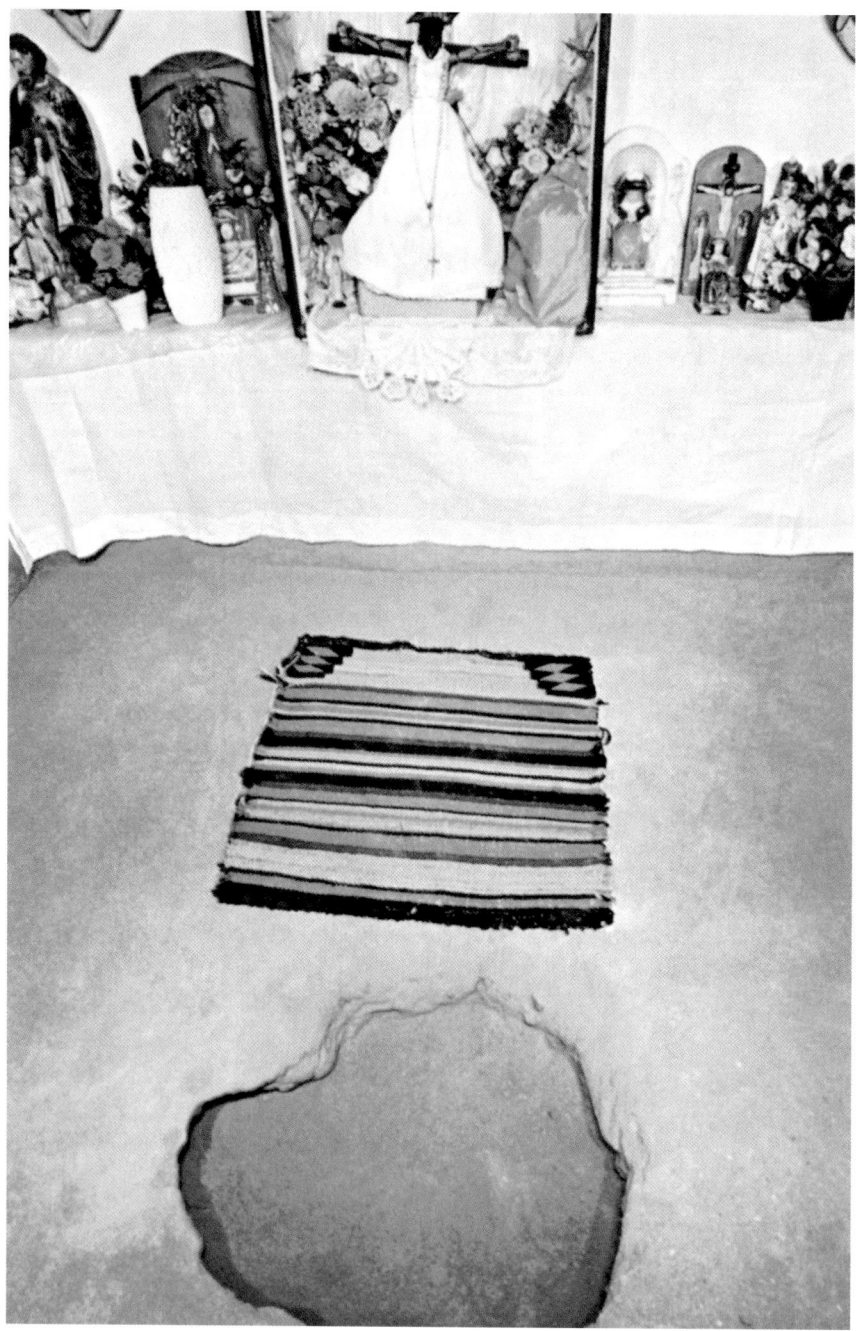

"*El Poso Sagrado* (The Sacred Hole)," Santuario de Chimayo, real photo postcard, unknown photographer, circa 1950. *Courtesy of the author*.

The history of dolls is most interesting. In ancient times, dolls were used in magic and religious rituals. Sometimes these effigies personified gods such as the Kachinas of the Hopi Pueblo Indians of New Mexico. They were supernatural intermediaries to be called upon in times of need. It took many centuries before dolls transitioned to being children's playthings. The popularity of puppets and puppet theater helped to create toy dolls. At first, very elaborate costumes, real teeth and human hair were used on puppets. Dolls went from being simple to ornate. There were ceramic dolls, as well as those made of wood and other natural materials. In New Mexico, Spanish colonial adults and children crafted dolls out of corn leaves and cloth. Through ingenuity, an industry was created, and dolls were sold and traded on the Santa Fé Trail. Children had a special attachment to their dolls. They named them and talked to them. Sometimes they claimed that their dolls answered them back, and they even protected them from *duendes*, or goblins.

In Spanish folklore, duendes were annoying mythical creatures that could lure boys and girls to disaster. In New Mexico, they said, "*Los duendes nunca duermen*" (Goblins never sleep). It was believed goblins lurked under beds, in closets and in dark corners. At night, they could attempt to clip the long toenails of unkempt children and mistakenly cut off their toes. Duendes at times would pull at uncovered feet as people slept. That is why bedding was tightly folded under mattresses for protection. These folkloric little monsters were the size of dwarfs and sometimes were accompanied by ghouls. These were spirits associated with graveyards. "*Allí van los señoritos derechos que van a acabar y a consumer*" (There go the upright little lords that will destroy and consume).

It was thought that in the shadows of the graveyards, there existed the undead, whose dominion was the cemetery. These undead are ghouls that are ever watchful and have huge, hollow eyes. From their realm of darkness, they curdle the blood when they are seen. If a black stallion stopped at a certain grave when being led through a churchyard in colonial New Mexico, a ghoul was said to inhabit it. A basin of boiling water was then poured into a hole near that grave. Holy water was also sprinkled onto the grave. European beliefs were prevalent in New Mexico. Added to this protection was the use of holy dirt from El Santuario de Chimayo. This was an ancient church said to have a hole with dirt that contained miraculous healing powers. No matter how much dirt pilgrims removed from the hole, it never emptied out. This is a mystery that unravels through the bone-chilling stories about misty figures and creatures from the past.

Night Walker—Thunder Mountain Goblin

Spanish pioneers in sixteenth-century New Mexico introduced Old World folklore and terrifying legends to the land. Native stories also evolved over time. A Pueblo Indian medicine man, or witch doctor, known as Popé organized a rebellion against the Spanish. In 1680, a Pueblo Indian revolt took place that forced the colonists to take refuge in an area called El Paso del Norte, the pass of the north. The colonists remained there until they were able to return to New Mexico in 1693.

Contrary to what most history books report, the 1680 Pueblo Indian Revolt in New Mexico was not the first time that Native Americans from different tribes in what we now call the United States united to fight against European settlers. The Spanish and the Pueblos lived in peace—except when they joined forces against others—up until the American occupation. The revolt of 1675 in the eastern part of the United States to attack English settlers, called the Great Swamp Massacre, united all but one tribe, which later joined due to attacks by the colonists. This was the first united Indian effort to expel Europeans. The massacre reduced the Wampanoags from fifteen thousand to four hundred who were held in prison camps. Other tribes located in English colonies had the same number of losses, with some tribes becoming extinct. By 1676, the English colonists had defeated the revolt of 1675. Many of the Native Americans who were not killed fled to Canada and the Southwest. In the same year is the first mention of the medicine man Popé. Written records of the time indicate Popé had been arrested by Spanish authorities in 1675 for practicing witchcraft and had been released. No other records, either through oral or written history, bring up Popé before this incident.

Popé simply appeared suddenly and had the gift of tongues. In other words, people listened to him and joined his ever-growing cult of followers. Under the guise of religion, he was able to convince others that drawing blood was their only way to salvation and freedom from a foreign culture. He set a time for murder. During the revolt, he and his followers terrorized the country and went on a rampage of killing, raping and pillaging. Pueblo Indian settlements that remained friendly with the Spanish and did not want to participate in the rebellion were decimated and burned to the ground. The ruthless leader demanded tribute from the remaining Indians, and he took many slaves and young maidens for his personal use. The former capital city of Santa Fé was his headquarters. During his successful revolt, he was instrumental in killing hundreds of Spanish settlers and countless Pueblo Indians in retribution. Native Americans who spoke Spanish or held on to anything that the Spanish had introduced were brutally murdered.

The Indians at Isleta Pueblo and other areas were so terrified by Popé and his men that they chose to follow the retreating Spanish to El Paso. Indian men, women and children numbering several hundred at Isleta fled with the Spanish and sought the protection of the Spanish military. Indians from other tribes also accompanied them. Word had already reached Isleta tribal leaders that Popé was decapitating and sacrificing anyone suspected of aiding the Spanish in any way. The ritual slaughter of innocent victims was out of control. No one was spared. When Governor Don Diego de Vargas recaptured Santa Fé in 1693, only half or fewer of the inhabitants of the ancient pueblo of Isleta returned with him. The others lived in so much fear that they stayed behind and established a new pueblo called Ysleta del Sur, or Islet of the South. It isn't known what happened to Popé, but by 1681, he was no longer in the picture; other Native American leaders had gained control. Popé simply disappeared from history.

Native American oral tradition makes no mention of Popé. He is known only through Spanish records. Out of the 1680 Indian Revolt, there arose a legend known as Thunder Mountain Goblin. A frightening story developed about a terrifying bogeyman that comes from the mountains and hides in attics or closets before appearing at night to snatch children and prey on its victims. This nightwalker is always waiting and watching.

As a *cibolero*, a buffalo hunter, Valentino Mendoza was afraid of only one thing. He couldn't stand the dark. Valentino was from La Liendre, a town in New Mexico that was settled in the 1840s by Spanish ranchers.

"Ruins at La Liendre," photograph by Lucía de Aragón, 1994. *Courtesy of the author.*

"*Carreta* (Ox Cart)," real photo postcard, Detroit Publishing Co., circa 1900. *Courtesy of the author.*

La Liendre, which means "a sting of nits," is now a ghost town and has no living residents. But the forlorn cemetery nearby has the remains of those who lived there, including Valentino. A few of the interred were victims of *liendres*, flesh-eating parasites. Liendres, in fact, are the eggs of lice, those flat-bodied, biting, blood-sucking insects that feast on animals and humans. They infest fur and hair and cause excruciating pain and suffering. They can grow large, and in La Liendre, they were especially big.

Once darkness arrived, they crawled out of the pillows and mattresses to feast on their sleeping victims.

Ciboleros were Spanish buffalo hunters who rode into the Llano Estacado, an area known as the Staked Plains in eastern New Mexico. They hunted buffalo herds to provide meat and hides for their hometowns. In the late 1600s, ciboleros used lances and sometimes crossbows to kill their game. Annual buffalo (bison) expeditions took place in October after crops were harvested and the weather was mild. Spanish ciboleros were legendary as expert horsemen who raced alongside stampeding buffalo, driving an iron lance with a twelve- to fourteen-inch blade into the buffalo's heart, dismounting and skinning the animal quickly. As many as one hundred men loaded fresh meat into *carretas*, which were wooden wheeled carts, bound for home. The fat of the animals was made into tallow for candles and cooking. Hides were tanned, and the skins were used as rugs and robes. Horns became utensils, and the long hair was used in mattresses for beds. Nothing of the animals was wasted.

Valentino loved to slice buffalo and beef into very thin translucent strips with his Spanish hunting knife. The knife and its razor-sharp, ten-inch broad blade with its riveted carved wooden handle was also a fierce weapon used to kill grizzly bears and for defense. The shining blade cut from both sides, and the young cibolero was an expert with its use. He peppered the slices of meat and strung them up to dry in the sun to make *carne seca*, popularly known as jerky. The Spanish word was actually *charkui*, but this sounded like "jerky." The process of making jerky was centuries old in Spain. When Valentino's ancestors ventured forth to the New World, they took loads of jerky and *galletas*, hardtack biscuits, for their long trip on the seas. This way they could sustain themselves with dried meat and dried bread on the voyages.

Once the ciboleros were back in La Liendre, the entire community held a fiesta to celebrate. They ate, sang and were merry. In a large *sala*, or dance hall, they did an exciting dance called a fandango on a hard-packed dirt floor smoothed out with sheep's blood, which resembled cement. The fandango was a Spanish dance in triple time. This was the progenitor of the now popular flamenco dance. The very spirited movements, which featured solos or couples, had been danced in New Mexico since the early 1700s. This triple-time dance included foot stomping, castanets and finger snapping. There was deliberate fast-paced footwork; eye-catching and dramatic clapping of hands, called *palmas*; and amazing actions that followed the guitars and sung *coplas*, which were improvised verses. Fandango was an old Spanish tradition living on in New Mexico. Quite often, the men had a contest of skill, and so did

"Dressed for the Fandango," real photo postcard, unknown photographer and date. *Courtesy of the author.*

the women. Valentino Mendoza was the most popular dancer and the undefeated champion in La Liendre. He loved to dance. He loved to sing, and he loved to drink the delicious wine produced in the local vineyards. There was plenty to eat, and the celebration lasted for days. But then it would be time to go home and go to bed.

Ever since Valentino was a little boy, his grandmother had told him stories. She told him tales of duendes, goblins that hide under the bed and in dark corners and then come out at night. Sometimes she would be washing clothes in the washtub, and he would sit down and listen to her. He knew about El Abuelo, which came out at night. *Abuelo* means "grandfather," but this certainly was not a typical grandfather. It was an old scary man, perhaps not alive, who went around in the darkness searching for children. His telltale signs were the sounds of the cracking of his whip and his terrible grunts. He dragged his feet and very stealthily looked around for boys and girls who should not be out late at night. No one knew what would happen

Goblin Belial, block print from *Das Buch Belial* by Jacobus de Teramo, Augsburg, 1473. *Courtesy of the author.*

if he caught him or her since they had never returned to talk about it. This was not the Nightwalker, though. This goblin was different. Not only did the Spanish fear him, but the Indians did, too. This goblin couldn't be seen. He was only heard and felt. They knew he was evil and could take your spirit. You would choke to death while lying in bed from fear. Valentino knew about goblins, ghouls and witches, but this one scared him the most—perhaps because his grandmother told him that when it was a windy night and thunder and lightning struck, this goblin came down from the mountains to claim those who were doing the wrong thing at night. A typical old fairy tale not to be believed, of course, so why was Valentino so afraid?

Valentino liked to party and have a good time. He was secure when he was with his friends and when he was drinking wine. He never thought about the future and was content with living for the moment. In fact, he had one big fault. Valentino took advantage of everyone and everything. He was also very selfish. He laughed at stories about the supernatural, but he actually enjoyed listening to them. One problem, though, was that he didn't like being alone, especially at night in the dark. He was afraid of his own shadow. He covered his fear up with others. Sometimes he kept candles lit, and he would be fine. When they would burn out, though, he was in trouble.

One night, Valentino was in bed and thought he heard voices from far away. A light breeze turned into a fierce wind. The shutters on the windows rattled. It seemed like the whole house was going to come down. Valentino got up and lit more candles. He didn't pray. That would be a last resort. He then heard thunder and saw lightning. The flashes cast vague images in the room. Then, one by one, the candles went out. Even though Valentino tried to relight them, they wouldn't stay lit. The poor man finally fell into an uncomfortable sleep. It was far into the night when he awoke. He had his eyes closed, but he knew someone was walking toward his bed. Valentino didn't want to look. Next, he could feel something near his bed. It brushed his hand. It moved up his arm. Valentino tried to scream for help, but no sound would come out of his mouth. He couldn't even breathe. They say Valentino died from fright that night. Everyone knew that too much of a good time at the expense of others would lead to a bitter end at the hands of a goblin that was more than willing to claim you as one of his own.

La Guajona—Vampire Witch

I was returning from a trip to Taos, where I had been looking for work. It was already getting late when I was heading home. There was a house that I had to walk by, and I was surprised when this very old woman saw me and called me. She said she needed help, so I walked up to her porch. She said, "Hijito, I have this trunk on the porch, and I have to get it inside the house, but it is very, very heavy." The nice old woman wore a long black shawl and a black dress that came down to her high-buttoned black shoes. Her kind face looked as endearing as anyone's old grandmother, so I said I would help her. I told her I was on my way home and had to get there before dark. She replied, "Oh, this won't take long. Someone big and strong like you can do this easily." When I tried to budge the heavy trunk, it was impossible to move. The poor old woman tried to help me, but both of us together couldn't do anything. "Never say never," she said. "I know we can do this. We just have to think. I've got it. I'll be back." She left and went into the house.

As I stood on the porch of this old house next to this heavy trunk waiting, I thought it was strange that I had never met this old woman. I must have passed through here a million times since I was a child, and I had never seen or met anyone at this house. I thought it had been abandoned long, long ago. It never occurred to me that anyone lived here. Anyway, the old woman finally returned, and she had this large broom she was carrying. "Pick up a corner of the trunk, and I'll put the broom under it and then we can slide it inside." I didn't think that would work. I struggled to lift it, and she quickly

"*Casa Vieja* (The Old House)," photograph by Santiago de Aragón, 2012. *Courtesy of the author.*

Opposite: "*La Dama* (The Lady)," Carte-de-Visite, unknown photographer, circa 1880. *Courtesy of the author.*

pushed the broom underneath the trunk and I let it go. It fell with a thud even though I had lifted it only a few inches. I pushed, and she pulled. I couldn't believe it! The trunk moved smoothly into the house.

We parked the trunk in the old woman's kitchen where she wanted it. I tried to leave, but she insisted she had to pay me for my kindness by offering me dinner. I knew I couldn't refuse her because, in my culture, it is very impolite to refuse something to eat and drink when it is offered. I was also pretty hungry since I had only eaten a couple peaches during the day—besides, what she had on the stove really smelled good. The old woman warmed up some freshly made tortillas and served me beans and green chile stew. She also had apple pie for dessert. That was my favorite. When she sat down, we talked.

The woman asked for my name, and I told her it was Fredolin Vigil. "What a nice name," she said. "Did you know that the surname Vigil comes from the word 'vigilant'? That means you have to be alert and watchful," she laughed. "My name is Guajona. Anyway, that is what they call me, and the name stuck since I was a child, so I know no other name. My, my, it's already dark outside. How time flies when you're having fun."

"*El Bosque* (The Forest)," real photo postcard, unknown photographer and date. *Courtesy of the author.*

Opposite: "*La Estufa* (The Stove)," photograph by Lucía de Aragón, 1992. *Courtesy of the author.*

"Oh God, I have to be getting home," I said. "It's going to be hard to see in the dark. I have to go through the *bosque* to get home, and there's no moon out."

"Forget about it. You have to stay here. You never know what creatures are out and about at night, and you won't live to tell if you wander out," she said convincingly.

I gave in. Besides, a good warm bed on a chilly night to me was way better then traveling through the bosque, where a wild mountain lion or bear could get me. The old woman had a little extra bedroom right by the kitchen. When I lay down, it was really nice and comfortable. It was like spending the night at my grandmother's. The mattress and pillow were so soft that I dozed off right away.

Around two o'clock in the morning, I woke up to talking in the kitchen. The old woman was throwing another log into the fireplace. With the fire, I could see clearly, but I couldn't see to whom she was talking. She kept saying the name Fujiyama, and a couple times I heard Jujuyana. But from where I was, I couldn't see anyone. Once, she glanced back into the bedroom, but I made loud snoring noises. Assured that I was asleep, the old woman walked up to a wooden shelf called an *alacena*. It had many containers, and she took down two small tin boxes. She sat at the table, rolled a cigarette and then quietly puffed away. The old woman was apparently meditating as she smoked. She got up from the chair and threw the remainder of the cigarette into the fire. Then she undressed and took the lids off of the boxes and applied something to her body. She returned the boxes to the shelf. Guajona did a strange little dance in which she took three steps to the right and three to the left. She then got into a tub of water she kept by the stove. The strange woman turned into an enormous bat and flew out through a window she had opened earlier. When she flew out, I got up and walked into the kitchen.

I went up and checked out the two tin boxes. They both had strange lettering, but I made out the words *UNTO DE DIFUNTO*. One said *DE HEMBRA*, and the other said *DE HOMBRE*, which mean "salve of dead female and male." They say "curiosity killed the cat," but I didn't believe anything like that. I was always curious and ready to try something new. I took my clothes off and applied the salve. I then did the little jig and got into the water as Guajona had done. Nothing happened. I was still Fredolin. I hadn't turned into a bat. I couldn't understand what the difference was. Then I noticed I had a religious medal of Saint Christopher that my nana had given me to protect me on my journey. I decided to take it off and tried the whole thing over again. This time I transformed into a bat (but not as big as her) and then flew out of the house.

As I flew out, I could see everything. The stars twinkled in the night sky. I felt so free and alive. Then I caught a glimpse of something far below. Someone was lying on the ground. It looked like a bat was clinched onto a person's neck. "It couldn't be..." I thought. "She's drawing blood." Suddenly, I felt like doing the same. Strangely, I craved blood, but I fought it with every ounce in my body. Guajona looked up. I knew she could sense that I was there and that I was not one of her own. I could see her evil eyes.

Even though I was a bat, I still had my mind and could think like myself. My grandmother taught me well. There are certain lines one doesn't cross. My immediate instinct was for survival, so I flew back to the house as quickly as I could. But just before I could fly in through the window, something grabbed me. It was a big, angry black cat. I knew Guajona's cat wanted to kill me and eat me. I fought it fiercely, but that cat was far stronger than I was. I didn't know what to do. I finally decided to go for its eyes, so I bit each one as hard as I could. It worked. The cat pulled away and ran off crying. I flew into the kitchen. I had seen how Guajona had transformed into a bat, but what I didn't know was how to change back.

I flew around and around the tank until I landed on the floor next to it because I was tired. Then I thought maybe I should do the little dance in reverse and move three paces to the left and then three to the right. I did this and jumped into the water. What a surprise! I turned back into myself. I immediately placed the saint's medal around my neck and got dressed. I high-tailed it out of the house as fast as I could. The sun was starting to peek over the mountains.

I got home and told my grandmother the whole story. My nana said that I had gone through an episode with La Guajona, the witch that converts herself into a vampire bat and preys on people and animals at night. She said I was lucky to get out alive and then reminded me that she had told me many times before, "*Sal de la casa y cuenta lo que te pasa* (Leave home and you will return telling about what happened to you). I hope you learned your lesson," she added. As I think about this, it seems like I was just having a bad dream or imagined the whole thing. But I know I really experienced it all, even though no one is going to believe it's true. I guess they will have to experience it on their own and learn the hard way, as I did.

La Llorona—Wailing Woman

Sometime in the seventeenth century, a group of Spanish colonists was traveling on the Camino Real de Tierra Adentro, the main road in New Spain, on their way to Santa Fé de San Francisco de Asís, the capital city of New Mexico. Marauding Indians attacked the group, which included men, women and children newly arrived from Spain. Most of the colonists escaped with their lives, but a few were killed. Those who died were buried on a hill overlooking a valley below, and large crosses were erected to mark the spot. The white-painted crosses were also intended to serve as a warning to others about the danger in the area.

These crosses were visible for miles around and became a landmark for weary travelers who journeyed for hundreds of miles to Santa Fé on foot and on horseback. Those journeying would stop near the crosses to pray for the repose of the souls of those who died. The place became known as Las Cruces, the crosses, and in time a Spanish military post, called a *presidio*, was established there to protect travelers and merchants.

This area, known as La Mesilla, a small, flat-topped hill or *mesa*, was a place of rich farmland. The Río Grande del Norte ran through there, so water was plentiful for crops. Mesilla eventually became a settlement with an outlying community known as Las Cruces. The Crosses is now a municipality with a major university called New Mexico State. Since a river and irrigation canals, called *acequias*, abound in the Mesilla Valley, many stories about a wandering wailing ghost that roams the waterways in an endless search for unsuspecting victims have evolved among the residents of Las Cruces since ancient times.

El Camino Real de Tierra Adentro, engraving, unknown engraver, circa 1840. *Courtesy of the author.*

Candelaria Valdez had grown up in Las Cruces hearing stories about La Llorona, the Wailing Woman. Candelaria is an interesting name. It means "Candlemas," a Roman Catholic Church fiesta, or festival, held on the second of February that celebrates the infant Jesus with his presentation in the temple. Candlemas is the fourth joyful Mystery of the Holy Rosary, a string of prayers in adoration of Mary, the mother of Christ. Mary is portrayed in Spanish art as La Virgen de la Candelaria. Whether in painting or in sculpture, she is sometimes pictured standing on a crescent moon holding the Christ child in one hand and a candle in the other.

According to legend, a miraculous statue was discovered on the island of Tenerífe in 1392. This island is one of the Canary Islands of Spain. This image, it is said, foreshadows the crucifixion and the sorrows of Mary at the death of her son. It is venerated to intercede in times of plague, droughts and epidemics.

In New Mexico, figures dressed as the infant Jesus drawn from this portrayal of Mary are taken to the church to be blessed. Candlemas also marks the end of the Christmas season and also traditionally signals the end of winter, as noted in the following rhyme:

If Candlemas be fair and bright come winter, have another flight,
If Candlemas bring clouds and rain,
Go winter, and come not again.

"Sangre de Cristo Mountain Crosses," unknown photographer and date. *Courtesy of the author.*

Chapel Altar, block print from *Histoires Prodigieuses*, Paris, 1597. *Courtesy of the author.*

    Candelaria Valdez was very proud of her name. Ever since she was a little girl, she had a special attachment to Mary, and she had a large *retablo* of Our Lady of Candelaria hanging on her bedroom wall. When Candelaria was about nine years old, her mother bought her a box of two dozen votive candles. She also gave her some small bottles to hold holy water. They took the candles to the church to have them blessed. Padre Vicente Saucedo at La Santísima Cruz Church, the Church of the Holy Cross, blessed the candles and filled the bottles with holy water. It would now be Candelaria's job to go from house to house and sell the candles and bottles of holy water. Her customers were mostly women who lived in houses near where she lived.

    Back in those days, all Hispanic residents in New Mexico had small altars that contained holy images of Christ and the saints. Of course, beautiful handmade crucifixes were the centerpieces, and sometimes pictures of the Sacred Heart of Jesus and the Sacred Heart of Mary were placed next to them. On a table leaned up against the wall were statues, candles and flowers. This was a central location in Catholic homes of the time to pray and meditate. Candelaria made *ramilletes*, bouquets of crepe paper flowers dipped in candle wax, for her household altar. She also sold some of the multicolored ramilletes she made. She learned the age-old tradition of needlepoint and quilting from her grandmother. Her nana knew all of the intricate designs that had been passed down in her family for generations, including the five-pointed star and many others.

Nana Soledad, Candelaria's grandmother, was a very superstitious woman. She also had a firm belief in the supernatural. She often told her granddaughter that if she looked into a well during La Noche de San Juan, St. John's Eve, she would see a reflection of her future husband and maybe a reflection of her first child. Candelaria hadn't tried it yet, and she kept putting it off. She also hadn't attempted to do another thing her grandmother had said. Her grandmother had told her to empty an egg into a glass of water and to place it under her bed. In the morning, she should check the glass and see what shape or form the egg had taken. This would foretell her future. For example, if the egg formed a skeleton or a coffin, this meant death. She also had her pray to her protector angel each night. She taught her grandchild to say:

> *Now I lay me down to sleep, I pray the Lord my soul to keep.*
> *Thy angels watch me through the night,*
> *And deliver me from evil till morning's light.*
> *If I should die before I wake,*
> *I pray the Lord my soul to take.*

Oh yes, Candelaria was scared by some things she learned, but she was also intrigued by others. Her grandmother would take burning cinders from the wood stove, place them on a metal plate and use it to purify the air in all the rooms of the house. She also liked to use *sensen*, an incense meant to purify the air. Nana Soledad believed in malevolent spirits and explained to Candelaria that if a candle flame burned blue, a ghost was nearby. Nana Soledad cautioned Candelaria by telling her the following story:

> Hay almas que andan penando, *there are souls in search of peace. Cención Varos is one of those lost souls trapped here on earth forever. The poor woman is doomed to wander at night. When she was alive, she lived in a part of Mesilla called El Barrio del Mal Ojo. Where she lived,* **Mal Ojo**, *or Evil Eye, was especially prevalent, and many infants died, which*

Kneeling Woman, nineteenth-century engraving, unknown artist. *Courtesy of the author.*

is how the place got its name. Mal Ojo can take place when someone stares into the eyes of a beautiful baby or child. You were very beautiful. You still are. Just before you were baptized, this man gave you the Evil Eye. You got very sick. You wouldn't stop crying, and you almost died. We finally got a hold of a Juan. Those with the name Juan have special powers. They can cure Evil Eye with their spit. You were cured.

When Cención Varos was born, she was promised to the son of Enrique Valles. Things were very different back in those days. When a couple had a son, the boy would be promised to the daughter born to a chosen family, and the new girl would be promised to him. Once she reached marriageable age, she would have to marry the one she was promised to, even if he was much older than she. This was a tradition dating back hundreds of years in our culture. This custom was meant to combine the wealth of livestock and land from two families into one for the future.

It turned out that Cención fell madly in love with a boy her own age. They always met in secret. He had been promised to another, so marriage between the two of them was out of the question. In time, Cención became pregnant and gave birth. She wound up having two children and was cast off as a village slut and called every name you can think of. The boy she loved married the one he was promised to at birth, so he was free and clear. Cención's own father kicked her out for bringing shame to his family name. One day, when Cención was washing clothes on the banks of the river, she began to cry in desperation. Her two children played in the water. It had rained in the mountains, so the water began to crest. When she turned to call her kids, she couldn't find them. She thought she saw them floating downriver, so she jumped in the river to swim after them. They say she drowned and that her pain-filled soul searches all of the waterways looking for her kids. Her chilling cries are sometimes muffled, but then they get louder and louder. They call her La Llorona, porque siempre llora *(because she cries for eternity). If she finds you playing in the river or ditches, she will take you thinking you are one of her children, and we will never, ever see you again.*

As a little girl, Candelaria was told not to play in the waterways. She and all of her school friends were interested in La Llorona. She heard many stories from people who claimed to have heard or seen her. Some swore up and down that the Wailing Woman almost caught them, but they miraculously escaped when they called for the santos to save them. Candelaria knew that the stories of La Llorona and others like it were meant to keep children in line. She also knew they were made-up stories and not real. She did enjoy listening to the spooky stories, and when she took classes in college, some of her class reports were about this Las Cruces folklore. One semester, she had to take an evening class and had to be at school until after dark.

It was getting late one night, and Candelaria looked at her wristwatch and began to get worried. She had a seven o'clock class at the university that should have been over hours before, but on this night, her professor was especially long-winded. It was her Southwest Studies class, and the teacher was lecturing about a topic he loved. He had researched superstitions among the Native Americans and the Spanish, and he knew everything there was to know about this subject. Candelaria was uncomfortable listening to his detailed ramblings. Her mother warned her that she should not get home late, but then Dr. Sabine opened up the class to questions, and this seemed to drag on forever. The poor girl couldn't sit still in her chair. She wiggled back and forth and sighed.

Earlier that day, Candelaria and her mother had gotten into a heated argument. They had a dispute over the subject of life and death. Candelaria argued that scientific fact is the only thing that one can go by and that something that cannot be seen, touched or felt simply does not exist. Once she got into college, she thought she was much smarter than her mother and especially her grandmother, who had never been able to go to school because she had to work all of her life, even as a little girl. Nana Soledad had grown up on a farm, where she and her siblings had to work from sunup to sundown. Once the argument got into the touchy subject of education, Nana Soledad had to cut in:

> *I know how to read and write, but experience is just as important.* Tu estás educada y desnucada. *You may be educated, but you haven't lived long enough to understand anything. Have your professors at the university lived the culture to be able to teach it? Or did they come from another culture, study us and now are the experts who tell us what our history, heritage and traditions are? Or did they read about our culture from someone who has their own perspective as to who we are and then put out another misinformed book about us? You have to learn how to think for yourself and not believe everything these people say or write. Yes, education is good, but think—remember who you are and why you are who you are! I know there is life after death. Period. End of discussion.*

While Candelaria sat in her class, she kept on reliving scenes of the argument in her head, as well as the last words her grandmother had told her. "*La Llorona te va a pescar por ser malcriada*" (The Wailing Woman is going to catch you for misbehaving and not showing respect). Finally, the class was over, and Candelaria could walk home.

It was quite late as she hurried along. Once she got home, she unlocked the door and rushed in, swung her schoolbooks onto a table and went straight to her room on the second floor. She didn't even hear her mother asking why she was so late. Candelaria was really tired. It didn't take her long to fall fast asleep. During the middle of the night, she woke up to the noise of scratching on her bedroom window. The noise was loud and unbearable. She was sure it was the neighbor's cat, which she thought was trying to get in from the cold. "*Maldito gato*," she yelled. "Shush you darn cat! I want to sleep!" The scratching continued. Candelaria finally looked toward the window and saw a hand reaching up. It was a thin hand with long, skinny fingers and long nails that gleamed in the moonlight. The nails scratched the windowpane. Then she saw a face peeking in. It was the face of an old woman with long white hair. The woman's peering eyes searched around the room and then, upon seeing Candelaria, gave her a deathly stare. Candelaria screamed at the top of her lungs. When she screamed, the face disappeared.

The frightened girl then thought it was only her imagination, so she got up and went over to the window. At first, she didn't see anything and was greatly relieved. But then she saw a woman standing near a tree. She was looking up at her. Then suddenly the woman's eyes turned glowing red, and two red beams of light shot up at Candelaria. The beams of light lit up her bedroom. As this happened, a piercing cry came out of the old woman's mouth. It was so loud that dogs down the street began howling. One deafening, piercing cry followed another. Now Candelaria was really scared. When Nana Soledad opened the door and flipped on the light to check on her granddaughter, Candelaria rushed into her arms, crying desperately. Nana Soledad embraced her and wiped away her tears as she told her about what she had seen. Her grandmother quietly listened. "*Que te dije*? What did I tell you?" she finally said. "I told you if you were not careful, La Llorona was going to catch you."

Lobisón—Attack of the Werewolf

Cleto Sotero lived in Ratón, New Mexico. *Ratón* has been interpreted to mean "mouse" or "rat." A story is told that when Hispanic sheepherding families settled the area sometime in the nineteenth century, a giant rat caused havoc in Ratón. They called it the "Goblin Rat" because it could be heard but was seldom seen. At first, people didn't know what was killing their lambs and chickens and destroying some of their crops. They laid traps, but nothing was caught. It wasn't until a small child went missing that the residents were really concerned. An armed hunting party searched everywhere but came back empty-handed. They followed a bloody trail, which led to a hole in the ground. They dug into the hole, which, after a few feet, came to an end.

One night, a coal miner who worked in the nearby coal mines heard something gnawing at his door. He lit a kerosene lamp and went to check. All he found were teeth marks he thought came from some animal that was searching for food and was trying to get in. He looked around and saw that the trapdoor to his cellar had been pulled off its hinges. He quietly walked down the steps that led into his cellar. He was stunned by what he saw—a black rat the size of a large dog hissed at him and flashed its hungry teeth. The miner could think only of trying to escape with his life. News about this incident spread.

What was really disturbing was that this horrible creature even struck at the local cemetery. Recently buried bodies had been mysteriously dug up; the remains were missing from the caskets, which were left open and

El Lobo (The Wolf), print from *La Doctrina Cristiana* (La Revista Catolica Publishing Co., Las Vegas, NM), 1899. *Courtesy of the author.*

strewn all over the ground. People were at their wits' ends as to what to do. They even had the parish priest use holy water and recite prayers on the location where they knew this monster had been. It appeared during the darkest parts of the night, so night watchmen were assigned in different sections of the town. There was even more intense fear when two of the watchmen disappeared from their posts, leaving only their rifles and other belongings behind. Then, as suddenly as the appearances and attacks began, they mysteriously stopped. Months and then years passed by with no more sightings or incidents reported.

Everyone knew Cleto Sotero roamed around whenever he wanted, even at night. His nickname was Peludo (Hairy). Cleto hated that name. Everyone called him hairy because he had hairy arms, hairy legs, hairy shoulders and a hairy chest. To top it off, he had long, scraggly black hair and an unkempt black beard. Cleto was the local handyman who did odd jobs around the community. They say he had been a very successful contractor who had built beautiful homes. He did all kinds of work. He was a jack-of-all-trades, an expert at plumbing, electrical work and framing. Cleto was also skilled at laying tile and rock. Then one day Cleto, for some strange reason, had a mental breakdown. He lost his profitable business and went bankrupt. He lost his home and his new truck. His wife and family left him. El Peludo, as he was now commonly called, slept under bridges, in alleys and on cardboard on the sidewalks, where he covered himself with spread-out cardboard boxes on cold nights. He found a wooden cart with a metal wheel someone had abandoned and used it to carry things he found.

People could hear this metal wheel screeching on the ground and knew when he was nearby. One of Cleto's favorite places was the town dump, where he would spend hours sifting through the trash searching for a treasure. Every now and then, he would find a food scrap to nourish himself and would devour it. Cleto was hired to build a stone wall around the cemetery to keep predators away. He was doing a great job building a five-foot wall, and the town fathers were really pleased with his work. During this time, he was covered in gray cement dust from head to toe, and he actually looked like a ghost walking around, especially at night. But once in a while, Cleto would mix his cement in a wheelbarrow and have it ready to apply. Then he would disappear, sometimes for days. When someone would go to check to see how he was doing, he would find the cement as hard as rock, with the hoe Cleto used to mix the cement stuck in it. When Cleto would finally return, he would spend hours breaking and removing the cement and then start all over again.

Whenever anyone had a plugged sewer line or any kind of dirty work to do, such as shoveling horse manure or cleaning chicken coops, Cleto was the one to call. They knew Peludo would crawl into the gutter, cover himself in poop and slime and not think anything about it. He always talked to himself and grumbled. No one gave much thought to what he was saying. He was just a harmless man to make fun of, and make fun of him they did. The kids often ridiculed him by calling, "Peludo Coludo" (hairy long tail). "We know you have a long tail like the garbage rat that you are," they would jeeringly remark. Both boys and girls thought it was great to poke fun at this poor, defenseless man. No one thought much of it—even the adults were used to making scornful, derogatory remarks about Cleto's clothes or how bad he smelled. Every now and then, Cleto would bathe in a ditch, so everyone

looked forward to that. When Cleto was paid for his dirty work, he would always go to the nearest liquor store and get a gallon of his favorite wine. He would find a hole to crawl into and drink until he was drunk.

One night, Cleto lost his way in the dark and wound up on a trail that led out of town. The poor handyman was in a drunken stupor. He saw a hill in the darkness and a large hole on the backside of the hill. He thought that this would be a good place for him to sleep. He crawled into the hole and felt something soft. Too drunk to be scared, he knew it had to be a nest made by some type of animal at some point. "Good," he thought to himself. "This will make a comfortable and soft place to sleep." Tonight, luck was on Cleto's side, as most of the time he slept on hard sidewalks. He drank more of his wine and quickly fell asleep, not giving another thought to the nest. Cleto had nice dreams. He dreamt of the day on which he and his brother had both married the women they loved. Then he dreamt of his children playing in the front yard of his house. His wife was busy in the kitchen preparing a meal. It had been a hard day at work, but he was really happy. He had never felt happier. It was a good life. He had plenty of money and security. He had a beautiful wife and great kids. Cleto had everything to live for. Then something nudged him. Drowsily, he looked and saw two eyes glaring and gleaming in the darkness. Thinking he was still living at home and his family needed to be protected, a fierce surge of energy went through his body, and a wild battle ensued. Days, weeks and months passed by, and Cleto never returned to town. People wondered what happened to him. He had simply disappeared.

"*La Cueva* (The Cave)," photograph by Ramón Juan Carlos de Aragón, 2011. © *Ramón Juan Carlos de Aragón*.

Opposite: "The Weddings," real photo postcard, northern New Mexico, unknown photographer, circa 1910. *Courtesy of the author*.

One night, when the moon was full and bright, a blood-curdling howl could be heard. Then there was dead silence. Suddenly, a yelping dog broke the silence. The people couldn't tell what direction the yelp was coming from, but they were sure the dog was being attacked and eaten by a wild animal. People in Ratón wondered if the Goblin Rat was back. Recently, many of the farmers had found dead lambs and chickens once again. But it was even stranger when a dead grizzly bear was discovered near a coal mine by the miners. It was partially eaten, and its throat had been slashed as if by long sharp claws. They wondered about what could have killed it.

Attack of the Werewolf, Johann Gruninger block print from *Die Emeis* by Johann Geiler von Kayserberg, Strassburg, 1517. *Courtesy of the author.*

Opposite: *Carrying Off a Child*, block print by Michael Furter, Basle, 1493. *Courtesy of the author.*

Stranger still was an empty casket found at the cemetery near a grave that had been dug up. The Goblin Rat was back to create havoc as it had before, and there was nothing they could do. Where would it attack next, and how many people would it kill? Everyone stayed locked up at night inside their homes and would only venture out when absolutely necessary. Panic and fear circulated around the town.

One night, by accident, someone caught a glimpse of the alarming wild killer. Someone brave enough to venture out described seeing a large gray-and-black wolf about the size of a cow. "It was really big," a man told his friends. "I have never seen anything like it before. It was carrying something in its mouth. I had a pistol, so I fired a shot into the air. That thing didn't even move. I fired another shot, and then you wouldn't believe what happened. You'll think I'm crazy, but it stood up on its hind legs to look over a bush it hid behind. From where I was, I could see it plain as day. Then it took off and disappeared in a flash." His compadres laughed. "Amigo, how much wine did you drink before you saw the creature?" one of them asked.

It wasn't a joking matter for very long, though. A couple was on their way home from Cimarrón on another night. They were traveling in their buckboard. Suddenly, their horse became very jittery and took off in a fast gallop. The wagon hit a large boulder and crashed, throwing its passengers onto some bushes and breaking apart the wagon. The couple rushed to move closer to the broken wagon to hide themselves from whatever was chasing them. Through the cracks of broken wood, they saw a giant wolf pounce on their horse. It tore away at the horse's flesh, ripping it apart. Every now and then, the wolf would stand up on its hind legs. And then it actually ran away like a man, carrying a chunk of the horse along with it. The couple found their way into town and told everyone who would listen what had happened. News about this spread around like wildfire.

Men armed with Winchester rifles riding on horseback and others with pitchforks tracked down what they called a "wolf-man," but they found nothing except for horse bones bearing strange teeth marks. They searched for days, but never at night. One of the trackers finally found Cleto living in a cave. He had become a hermit, preferring to live by himself rather than be around people who always laughed at him. As for this Lobisón, or wolf-man, it continued appearing under the cloak of darkness, attacking unsuspecting victims. They claim it still comes out once in a while. But this strange creature has moved on to other parts of New Mexico, appearing in Trementina, Ojo Caliente and Peñasco.

PART II
THE UNDEAD

Historical Overview

There were a few ancient medieval phrases once prevalent in New Mexico that appear to have disappeared from common use. One was "*almas agonizando*," which literally means "a soul that is in agony or is agonizing." But the way it was used referred to someone close to dying. The popular belief was that days or weeks before someone was about to die, his or her spirit had the ability to roam. The man or woman could appear in various places; he or she could be mysteriously seen for a moment before vanishing. In addition to foretelling their death, it also gave them the ability to see people they knew or loved one last time. They could also see places they cherished in their hearts before moving on. The other phrase was "*almas que andan penando*." The word *penando* comes from *pena*, which means "sorrow" or "pain." The folk translation of the phrase is "souls in search of peace." If a person died unrepentant, in sin or without receiving the Last Rites, then that individual could not travel to the next world to be in peace and happiness.

The soul's being trapped here on earth or existing in the netherworld meant the spirit could go back and forth into the natural world, appearing where it had existed before in life. Many people believe that, at times, one can catch a glimpse of this apparition, which is dead but still lives. Paranormal activity among these spirits includes poltergeists that can move furniture, rattle dishes and walk by while only their footsteps are heard, or they can be seen sitting in a chair or simply standing. People once had such a preoccupation with or fear of this phenomenon that they chiseled "Rest in

Peace" (RIP) onto tombstones. They hoped and prayed that the spirit of this person would not return. In New Mexico they always said, "*Que Dios lo tenga en su verdadero descanso*" (May God keep him in his true rest).

In the past, people in the villages and towns of New Mexico did not have the luxury provided by morticians and funeral homes. Embalming was a scarcity. Family, friends and relatives handled all the arrangements for burial when someone died. Pinewood coffins were hand built. The women decorated them. Wakes were held in the homes of the deceased. Large receptions took place after the burials. It was not uncommon to hear someone saying, "*Lo enterraron antes de tiempo* (They buried him before time)." How did they know? Premature burials were often the topic of conversation.

The subject of premature burials became so widespread that safety coffins were invented. The first recorded use of a safety coffin was in 1792, when Duke Ferdinand of Brunswick ordered that, upon his death, the coffin he was placed in should have a lock installed and a key placed in his pocket in case he should need it. He also asked for a window to let light in and an air tube. Due to premature burials during the eighteenth and nineteenth centuries, many safety measures were developed, invented and patented. These included the use of bells, cords, breathing devices and other items that were installed in coffins or placed in tombs. Therefore, it was not unusual

Death Calling, J. Frellon print from *Imagines Mortis* by Hans Holbein the Younger, Lyons, 1547. *Courtesy of the author*.

Opposite: *Undead Rising*, block print by A. Aubrey, Germany, 1604. *Courtesy of the author*.

for a body to be exhumed, such as the following incident that occurred in New Mexico.

Sometime in the fall of 1925, Sevedeo Ortiz purchased a large family burial plot in Mount Calvary Cemetery in Las Vegas, New Mexico. That was where his father and mother were buried. It wasn't long before Sevedeo had a problem to deal with. His grandmother Ursulita Rael was buried in another section of the cemetery, one that was located far away. On Memorial Day, as he cleaned the grave sites, he thought long and hard about what he could do. As Sevedeo pulled weeds and cleared trash that had blown onto the graves, he came to a decision. Sevedeo decided to have his grandmother's coffin dug up and moved to the family plot.

It was a clear, sunny day with only a few clouds in the sky when the work was started. Three strong men armed with shovels dug into the hard-packed dirt as Sevedeo impatiently looked on. Time dragged on as the men dug deeper and deeper. It seemed as though his grandmother was buried more than six feet deep. Shovels of dirt piled up high until a thud was finally heard. The coffin had been struck. It took some effort to get the weathered casket to the surface. Sevedeo had to help. Once it was on top of the ground, the loving grandson thoughtfully gazed at it. Then he suddenly told his workers to open the gray coffin. The workmen strenuously objected, but he was able to convince them to do it for him. For some unknown reason, he wanted to see her. As the lid creaked open, Sevedeo stood there in shock when he saw the body. She had been buried alive. Her tortured hands were raised up, and her fingernails were broken and filled with caked blood. Her wretched mouth was wide open in a silent scream. Her peppered white hair was torn at the roots. The cloth inside the casket lid was in shreds. There were deep scratches and gashes on the hinged cover that served as a testimony of terror and pain. One cannot even begin to imagine what it would have been like to wake up in a black tomb. But unbelievable as it might sound, some people have escaped the grasp of death from the grave.

During times of war, premature burial was used as a means of torture and execution. The Jewish Holocaust and the Bataan Death March during World War II are prime examples of this. The majority of the soldiers who composed the 200th Coast Artillery were Hispanics from the towns and villages of New Mexico. In December 1941, it was this unit that arrived first to defend the islands of Luzón and Corregidor and the harbor defense forts of the Philippines. The New Mexicans fought with very little food, no medical help, outdated equipment and virtually no air power. On April 9, 1942, Japanese forces captured the soldiers. After their capture, the Japanese marched them for days in the sweltering heat, with thousands dying from disease, starvation, lack of water, torture and murder. Many more died in the horrendous conditions of the confinement camps. Of the 1,800 New Mexican soldiers of the 200th Coast Artillery, approximately 800 returned to New Mexico. One of these survivors was José S. "Chaveta" Chavez from Valencia County, New Mexico, who was buried alive twice. He told the story of his burials:

> *The Japanese threw me into a grave, and dirt was thrown over me and the rest of the dead, decaying soldiers. I don't know how, but I managed to crawl over many dead bodies and saw a light opening at the top of the grave. It took me two hours, but I made it out. The Japanese were totally stunned. My buddies carried me back to the barracks. Two weeks later, they buried me again. It began to rain, and I came back to life.*

"A Death in Adelino, New Mexico," photograph by José Calles, 1948. *Courtesy of the author.*

Le Mort, Heiligtumbuch, block print by Hernach, Vienna, 1502. *Courtesy of the author.*

The Undead

The soldiers who survived World War II and other wars kept mementoes or souvenirs to remind them of what they endured. The families of the deceased loved ones kept photos, letters and anything else they could to keep the memories alive. It was extremely hard to let go, and for some strange reason, it was thought that the information they received could be wrong and that those who were taken away so soon would some day walk in the door or be seen in a familiar place. Many claimed they had caught a glimpse of them.

They say that old habits die hard. A tradition passed down for centuries was the keeping of a *memento mori* or a *recuerdo del difunto*. This was keeping of mementoes to serve as reminders of the person who had passed on. This would include a lock of hair or a favorite garment that the deceased had worn. For a time, hair was the favored memento. It was placed into elaborate lockets or picture frames. It was also woven into intricate folk art pieces. A favorite uniform, dress or coat was passed down. A particular family would hold on to these loving keepsakes for generations. It was felt that a part of those long gone stayed with these mementos. The advent of photography brought about the bizarre practice of taking pictures of the dead. Most of the time, it was a final image of the person in the coffin before burial. But other times, the dead were propped up on chairs or on beds to have a picture taken before an undertaker's hearse would arrive. If a child or an infant died, the mother held it on her lap and covered his or her head with a shawl. This gave the overall setting a ghostly look. It was especially sinister when a doll was placed in the hands of a girl or when a woman was shown holding a bouquet of flowers. Native Americans feared photographers. They thought they had the power to capture their spirit in a photograph. The Indians felt that if they lost their spirit, they would not remain whole. When they died, part of them would stay behind and could not move on to the afterlife or happy hunting grounds. Many world cultures believe that both benevolent and malevolent beings exist among us and that they appear and are heard most often after dark. These creatures toy with our lives. Perhaps they can cross over from one plane of existence to another and either help us or hurt us. At times, they may even walk among us.

Santa Compañía— Holy Company

The dark cemetery had such a compelling allure for Roberto and his friends. Roberto, Pablo and Andrés lived near the ancient *camposanto*, the graveyard, called El Aposento Sagrado (The Holy Habitation). Although this ominous resting place of the departed was encircled by a red stone wall built in the late 1700s, the three boys devised an ingenious plan to scale it. There was actually a double wall. The wall, lined with desert weeds and old trees, that ran along the cemetery property line was easy to climb over. Once inside, the solemn crosses and the cold, stark tombstones of the hallowed space lured the young explorers. "Mira! Look!" shouted Pablo. This man was born in 1832 and died in 1934!" "Madre de Dios!" yelled Andrés. "That's over a hundred years!" Roberto said, "Look at this one. This little girl died at nine, it says, from smallpox!" All three noted that most of the inscriptions read "Requiescat en Pace" (Rest in Peace). Suddenly Andrés animatedly pointed to a stone and said, "This one says 'RIP.' Doesn't that mean to tear up?"

"No estúpido, that means rest in peace—or is it pieces? Well, something like that," answered Roberto. "They just put the first letter of each words."

Andrés jumped in, "Oh, now I know what RIP means."

One of the largest tombstones had enough space for the three of them to sit as they wondered about what lurked beneath their feet under the ground. They came up with some pretty wild stories. Roberto saw a mysterious hole

"*Camposanto*," New Mexico Spanish colonial cemetery, real photo postcard, unknown location and photographer. *Courtesy of the author.*

"Adobe Wall Enclosure," photograph by Santiago de Aragón, 2012. *Courtesy of the author.*

San Miguel del Bado by C.B. Granam, circa 1848. *Courtesy of the author.*

near one of the graves and said he had heard it was a sure sign that the one buried there was a vampire. A vampire that could only find rest if you poured boiling water into the hole just before it would come up as the sun set and the full moon rose.

All three of the boys were startled when they heard mysterious music and something fluttering in the trees. It turned out to be a black crow. Any slight movement caught their attention, but they would feel self-assured and laughed when they would see a horned toad or a scampering squirrel. Roberto was the bravest of the three, so he liked scaring his friends. "My abuelita told me that evil spirits could take over the bodies of dead people," he said.

"Really?" said Andrés, who was the most timid of the three.

"Sí, she said they become the walking dead possessed by the spirits."

"Ay, Dios mío. Maybe we shouldn't be here. It's getting late—we should go home!"

Roberto continued:

> *My grandma told me never to be out at night without garlic for protection. She said that once there was this man named Antonio Quintana who worked in the beet fields of Las Vegas near the Río Gallinas. He fell off a wagon on his way home and broke his neck. He died. They had a* velorio del difunto, *a wake for the dead, at his widow's house. His body was laid on the kitchen table, and lit candles encircled it. After they finished praying the rosary, my nana said all of the* dolientes, *mourners, went home. Some of the Penitentes from San Miguel sang the* alabado *"La Encomendación*

del Alma," which was commending the poor man's soul to heaven. After the Penitentes left, the ones chosen to spend the night in vigil near the body stayed praying. My nana Emilia said they were praying to the holy image of Nuestra Señora del Refugio, Our Lady of Refuge, who saves everyone who prays to her from the fires of hell. She was the patron saint of the family since Quintana's wife was named Refugio.

A la media noche, at midnight, when the flickering candles were casting ghostly shadows on the walls, those praying suddenly saw a dark figure on the partially illuminated walls. My nana's exact words were, and I'm only repeating what she said, "Antonio Quintana sat up and was staring wide-eyed and pale-faced trying to speak to the mourners, who screamed out at the top of their lungs in fear." She said that this was the first time that Antonio Quintana died.

"You're lying," Andrés said.

"No I'm not," said Roberto. "Cross my heart and hope to die if I'm lying. It's the God's honest truth. That's what my nana told me." Then he went on with his hair-raising story:

The second time he died, he was already in his mid-nineties. She said Quintana loved to ride his gray horse Murrieta. One day when he was out checking his alfalfa fields, the horse threw him. His ranch hands found him on the ground. Old Antonio Quintana wasn't breathing, and once more, he was pronounced dead. This time my grandma said they had the velorio *for two days to make sure he was dead.*

On the way to the camposanto, *Padre Gallegos and the people stopped to pray at all of the* descansos. *At the resting places, they placed a cross for the deceased man with the rest of the crosses as they carried the coffin to the cemetery. My nana told me that as everyone got to the grave site, they laid the coffin down and knelt to say a final prayer of farewell. This was a silent prayer meant to come from the most inner thoughts from those who had known Quintana during his life. As they all meditated, they heard a very faint knocking noise that steadily got louder. It came from the pine coffin. When some of the men finally got the courage to open the coffin, Antonio Quintana sat up and gave them all a deathly, cold, blank stare. Quintana actually lived to be over a hundred. The strangest thing was that people wound up fearing him. They said that every time he walked into a house, someone in that house would die soon after. They cautioned he was one of the walking dead. One day during*

"*Sepultura* (The Grave)," photograph by Santiago de Aragón, 2013. *Courtesy of the author*.

the feast day of San Juan Nepomuceno, which was the first time that the saint's day had been celebrated in San Miguel, Antonio Quintana keeled over and finally fell dead for good.

A deathly silence fell over the three of them as Roberto finished his story. Pablo broke the silence. "Wasn't that the first tombstone we saw with that name over there?" he asked. All three of them turned and looked back toward the grave of the man who lived to be over one hundred. Pablo and Andrés jumped off the tombstone they were sitting on and started to run away. Roberto was surprised with their reaction and yelled out, "There's nothing to be afraid of. The sun's still out. Don't be chickens!"

Pablo and Andrés couldn't hear a thing. They both scaled the wall as though nothing was there and raced home. Roberto felt pretty confident since the sky was blue and the sun was still bright in the cloudless sky. It was a beautiful day, and the breeze felt comforting as it brushed his face. He thought this place was a great place to rest for eternity. He felt so relaxed that he decided to take a little nap before heading home. He got down from the tombstone, walked away from the graves and found a nice spot with soft, loose dirt on which to lie down. He soon fell into a deep, deep sleep, and not even the dead could have woken him. When the boy sleepily opened his eyes, he saw the full moon up above and the black darkness of the sky. Roberto felt a cold breeze, and he smelled bees' wax in the crisp air. He quickly got up and, seeing light, turned and saw people holding lit candles and staring at him. One of the living dead, or undead, placed a cross in his hand, and Roberto, now horrified, remembered the rest of his Nana Emilia's story about La Santa Companía. She told Roberto that if one of the living was found wandering around the cemetery at night, La Santa Companía gave that person the duty of leading the procession. Poor Roberto now joined the procession of the dead as its leader to the end of the world. Roberto always knew he would have to pay for his sins, but he didn't know it would be this way. He hadn't thought about his nana's warning: "*De la suerte y la muerte no hay nadie quién se escape!*" (Of luck and death, there is no one who escapes!)

Dead Ringer

It was the twilight of the couple's lives, but they gloated in the attention as everyone snapped pictures of them. It was their sixty-fifth wedding anniversary, and they had renewed their vows at their parish church of San Felipe. Amado Leyba was dressed in his best black suit. He carried his black hat neatly tucked under his arm and proudly showed off his sparklingly polished black boots. His wife, Soledad García Leyba, beamed with delight in her very nice cream-colored wool knit dress adorned with a fancy gold-colored, flower-shaped brooch studded with ruby-colored oval stones and imitation pearl necklace with matching earrings. Her cheeks glowed with the rouge she had applied that morning, and the aroma of her strong perfume filled the church. She had calluses and arthritis on her toes, but she beared the pain of her new beige, small-heeled shoes. The front cover of the ceremony's booklet had a picture of them as a young married couple, and within the booklet were many pictures of their children, grandchildren and great-grandchildren.

During the wedding ceremony, the elderly couple humbly listened as Father Cleofes Baca addressed those present by saying, "Amado and Soledad serve as a very good example of a genuine couple that is devoted to the church and to their marriage. They have been *mayordomos* cleaning and caring for our church of San Felipe and have been faithful servants. I have to say Amado never fails in helping clean the weeds at the camposanto each year. Our cemetery is a thing of beauty because of him and his compadres." Father Cleofes continued, "Soledad and her comadres always provide

"*La Pareja* (The Couple)," photograph by James N. Furlong, circa 1910. *Courtesy of the author.*

Opposite: San Felipe de Neri Church, Albuquerque, New Mexico, Continent Stereoscopic Co., circa 1880. *Courtesy of the author.*

delicious chili, beans and good tortillas for the workers. No one makes tortillas like Soledad's. You young couples out there should be so lucky to have a long marriage as theirs." When the good pastor got to the "I do's," Amado and Soledad both said, "I do" before Father Baca could ask the question. The wedding guests laughed out loud as he teased the couple. The elderly couple was used to the pastor's sense of humor, and they laughed along with everyone. After the ceremony, the congregation clapped with joy as Amado and Soledad stood before them.

The reception was held in the beautiful enclosed patio of San Felipe, and the dance continued at the park across the street from the church, where all the fiestas took place. The band played from the large gazebo at the center of the park. When Amado and Soledad weren't dancing to the music of Los Abeytas, they talked about their early years and how different things were when they were growing up compared to society today. Amado said proudly, "I have twelve children and so many grandchildren and great-grandchildren I can't even remember their names. But I love them all. Just the other day, when I was talking, with Vicente Fernandez…" Soledad quickly interrupted,

"Amado, Vicente Fernandez died two years ago, that is not the other day, *a que hombre*." Amado, giving his wife a glare, continued, "Yes, I know. As I was saying, the other day when I was talking to Don Vicente, one of my great-grandchildren came up to me, and I couldn't remember his name. It's Uno. I knew it was something unusual. Then I remembered asking my granddaughter Josefa when he was born. 'What kind of a name is that?' She immediately clarified to me that she named him Uno because he was born first, Number One.' I quickly asked, 'So your second child will be named Number Two?' My response did not go well." Soledad quickly jumped in, 'Amado, you talk too much, *como hablas*!'"

The following day after the ceremony, Amado and Soledad rested at home. They talked about the great time they had and how blessed they were to have such a wonderful family and so many good friends. They looked at all the gifts piled high on a large table against the wall. They each opened boxes and showed each other what was inside. It seemed they had gotten everything under the sun from silver frames for their photographs to tools for working outside in their flower garden. Everyone knew how much the elderly couple loved gardening and working on their house. Their house was spotless, and everything was in its place. Soledad spent every day cleaning the house. She thought of that as her job, and she was very proud of it. She liked the compliments she got from family and friends and other visitors. She couldn't stand seeing something out of place nor seeing a speck of dust. The floors, which she washed two to three times a week, were always shiny. After Amado retired from the railroad, they both worked together inside and outside. Soledad was never happy with the way he did things inside the house, but the yard and small garden were always free from any weeds. The yard outside was like the house inside, immaculately clean.

Finally, they were down to their last two gifts, which were the smallest. "What could be in these, Soledad?" Amado asked. "No sé, I don't know," Soledad answered. "Open yours first, Amado," she told him. Amado very carefully took off the wrapping paper and placed it neatly on the pile that Soledad was saving. They never wasted anything and still had things in the house they had saved when they were a young bride and groom. When Amado took the lid off the box, he found a small object inside. "What's this?" he asked. After checking it out, they saw it was a cellphone. "Open your present," he told his anxious wife. She very carefully unwrapped her gift and also found a cellphone inside.

Their children had insisted for some time now that it was important for their parents to have cellphones. "You never know when something is going to happen," they said. But they had not given into their children's requests. It just seemed so crazy that people couldn't have conversations anymore without a phone in their hand or checking out their phone for text messages. Well, there was nothing they could do about it now. They both searched for tags to see who had given them the new phones, but they didn't find any. They knew it had to be their children. Their money would be wasted, so they would have to use them once they learned how.

The couple began putting everything away. Soledad cooked lunch while Amado tried to figure out how the phones worked. He couldn't—it was a mystery. Later in the day, one of the phones began to ring from where it was placed on the coffee table. Amado picked it up. He lifted up the top, and he could hear the faint voice of their eldest daughter. He repeatedly said hello, but she continued to say, "Mom, Dad, can you hear me?" "It doesn't work! She can't even hear me," he said loudly. Soledad joined her husband in saying hello. "We can barely hear you," she said. Their daughter asked, "Are you sure you have the right side of the phone up?" Soledad took the phone from Amado. She turned it around and put it to her ear. "Hello!" she yelled. Their daughter was laughing. Soledad could hear her now. Elena finally stopped laughing and said, "You guys are too much. You must have had the phone upside down." "Well, we're not used to these things," Soledad stated. "Mom, I'll be there later this afternoon to show you and Dad how to use your new phones. *Bueno,* " their daughter responded and hung up. "So what do we do now?" Soledad asked. "How do you hang up the phone?" "Just close the thing and they can do it when they get here," Amado responded in frustration.

Elena showed up as she had said. She showed them that numbers for family and friends, including the children, were all listed under contacts. "All you do is click on 'contacts.' Then scroll down and find the person you want to talk to, click on their name and then the green button. It's that easy. Just close the phone or click on the red button to hang up. Of course, you have to have the right side up!" she said laughing. "*Malcriada!*" Soledad responded.

Amado and Soledad spent the next few days playing with their new toys. She would call him and he her, even if they were in the house. If he was in the bedroom and she was in the kitchen, he would call her to ask where his favorite shirt or his other things were. When he was outside, instead of opening the door and calling her like he had done thousands of times before, he simply clicked her number, and she was there instantly. He used the phone to ask her when breakfast, lunch or dinner was ready. At nighttime, when they went to bed, he would call her and say goodnight just to tease

Soledad. While watching TV, both Amado and Soledad kept their phones nearby. They seemed to spend more time alone since their children would call instead of coming over for a visit. When Amado would misplace his phone, he would go into a panic. Soledad would ask, "Did you take it with you when you went to the bathroom or when you were working outside?" "Yes," he would say. "But I had it when I called you a little while ago." They would search everywhere until Soledad would think of calling his number with her phone, and then they would find it.

One day, Amado got up very early to work in the yard. He cleaned a little and then piddled around in his garden. He meticulously searched for the smallest weed, pulling it from its tiny roots. He felt great satisfaction gathering up these baby weeds in a pile. Amado looked at his tomato plants, his chile plants and his *calabacitas*, which were his prized pumpkin plants. He tenderly took care of his calabacitas because his favorite meal was fresh fried green pumpkin, which his wife carefully prepared with onions and corn. His mouth would water just thinking about it. He knelt at his garden, picturing what was to come when the plants were ready to be picked, when he suddenly felt dizzy and a sharp pain in his chest. Amado fell forward on the ground, and he pictured himself at a wake, a funeral and then being buried in the ground, as his eyes rolled around in their sockets. He remembered when he was young. His whole life passed in front of him. He saw the Grim Reaper impatiently waiting for him with a broad smile.

Amado thought he was ready for this day, but this was so sudden. He and Soledad had everything prepared. They had their plots ready at the cemetery, their coffins were paid for and the tombstones were engraved with everything but the final day of their lives here on earth. The old couple prayed their rosaries every night before going to bed and every morning at five o'clock sharp. He remembered his cellphone. It was in his left pocket, where he always kept it. Amado painfully managed to reach for it, and he called his wife for help. Luckily, Soledad heard the phone and answered it. Within seconds, she went rushing out of the house, frantically searching for her poor husband. She screamed, *"Ay Dios mío,* Amado. What happened?" Amado weakly answered, "I don't know" and then passed out.

Next, Amado found himself on a hospital bed with an IV attached to his right arm. Dr. Chavez was standing next to the bed. "Am I dying?" Amado asked as he struggled to open his bloodshot eyes. "Of course not," the doctor answered. "You're probably going to live to be 110." Laughing, the good doctor added, "You're probably going to bury all of us." You should have seen how relieved and happy Amado was. He and Soledad hugged and kissed for joy. During the following weeks, Amado told everyone who would listen that the doctor told him he had the body of a much younger man, that he was in amazing health and that he was going to live to be 110. "I guess I'm going to be like my uncle Cipriano, who was 109 when God remembered him and called him," Amado exclaimed.

It turned out that a couple months later, Amado was once again working in his garden tending his plants when he got a severe pain in his chest. He had taken his allergy pill and an acid reducer because he always loved eating hot chile, which he had for breakfast, lunch and dinner. He reached for his cellphone in his pocket, but then he remembered he had left it in the restroom when he was washing his hands. He couldn't call Soledad, so he started to panic. In the meantime, Soledad was busy cooking in the kitchen and hadn't noticed Amado hadn't come back into the house. When she called Amado in for dinner and he didn't answer, she thought he was asleep in the bedroom, since he often took naps during the day. He wasn't there. She thought he might be working on his car in the front yard, but she didn't find him there either. Finally, she decided to call his cellphone and found it in the bathroom. Now she was really worried. She called out, "Amado!" at the top of her lungs and ran like crazy while searching everywhere. She found him lying flat on his back, hidden by a bush. Soledad was hysterical. Her beloved husband was dead.

It was a very sad funeral at the San Felipe Church. Soledad, who never showed much emotion when others died, cried without consolation for her beloved husband. "Amado, Amado, what am I going to do without my Amado?" she sobbed. She was torn remembering Father Cleofes's words when he presided at hers and Amado's wedding, "Till death do you part." She didn't want to believe that her husband could be gone. How could death be the end? She did not want to let go. At the burial site, Soledad looked on in anguish as the gray casket that encased Amado's cold body was lowered slowly into the hungry ground. She heard a loud thud when the coffin hit the bottom. Benjamin Romero, the funeral director, announced to the crowd it was time to leave and gather back at San Felipe with the family to share in a meal and tell stories of remembrance in honor of Amado. Soledad asked her family and friends to please leave the grave site and give her some time alone in prayer with her husband. Everyone left after tossing a flower into the hole, which now held Amado's body encased in his casket. With a final farewell, the grief-stricken old woman tossed a red rose that silently and very slowly drifted into the gaping, chilling hole. Soledad looked painfully away at the ominous tombstones in the shivering cemetery as the heartless gravediggers

"*Camposanto* (Cemetery)," photograph by Santiago de Aragón, 2013. *Courtesy of the author.*

shoveled in the black dirt. Suddenly the empty silence in Soledad's mind was broken by the annoying sound of a phone. Her cellphone was in her leather purse, but it only served to bring back painful memories of her beloved husband and his constant calls throughout the day. Soledad didn't want to hear it, so she desperately sought to ignore it—especially after it rang for a second series of drawn-out rings and then a third. She finally reached into her purse to pull it out. Soledad flipped the pitiless cellphone open to see who had called. It showed Amado's number.

Soledad's instinct was that her husband was alive, so she ordered the gravediggers to stop and pull out the coffin. She had put Amado's phone inside his suit pocket before they closed the lid to the coffin. It seemed as though it took forever for the coffin to be brought back up to the surface. Soledad was frantic. When the lid was pulled up, she was disheartened to discover that her husband was indeed dead—but why was the phone in his hands? She had put it into his pocket. She was startled when her phone rang again. Soledad flipped her phone open and put it up to her ear. In disbelief, she heard Amado's voice saying, "I love you, and I will wait for you." The poor woman then fell over dead with both phones in her hands. At San Felipe, the family waited for Soledad. The funeral director entered with the sad announcement of what had happened. Suddenly, everyone was reaching for their phones as they all rang in unison. Some phones rang with music, others with the everyday phone ringtones and still others with the words "You have a call from Soledad…You have a call from Soledad…" The mournful cries of Amado and Soledad's children began.

Bibiana

I know not how it all began. It was a mausoleum cold and distant. Pounding heart, veins with tension, short of breath and withered mind. I walked along the tombstones gathered, dates of death and souls long gone. Undead gathered, calling to me. But I turned away in fear and fright. But curious and full of wonder, I looked afar and saw a house. It was so haunted; it was calling. I roamed the passageways and corners, and with turning eyes, I strained to see. I saw the ghouls and frightening specters reaching out to call me in. It was a feeling of someone watching, someone invisible and yet right there. Right behind me, to the side, in my mind I tried to hide. Forlorn images of those long gone pleaded out to me in despair. Movements in the shadows haunting, at midnight I yearned for morn. Dark and moonlit corridors I traveled while falling rain and thunder struck. Doorknobs turning, chambers glowing, I turned around and saw her there. Standing at an ancient graveyard where vampire witches haunt and roam, a chiseled tombstone spelled her name: BIBIANA. "May She Rest in Peace? She lived for love." How can I describe this feeling? I pulled away, but yet I was drawn. On this dark and dreary night, I fell into a deep, deep sleep. I suddenly awoke as I was kissed by the lips of death.

In my poverty what do I have tonight when I died yesterday? I only have what I do not have. The hours I lived yesterday. But so uncertain that I am of what I will be tomorrow that I will not say it because I died tonight. Crying for the absence of Bibiana, the night finds her and the sun leaves her, adding always passion to passion, memory to memory, pain to pain.

"*Mujer* (Woman)," nineteenth-century tintype photo, circa 1886. *Courtesy of the author.*

Who would want her? Who would love her? Her testimony of love is like an arrow in my heart, a verdict of my impending doom. On this road of my journey is a resting place full of terror and torment. A scythe gleams in the moonlit night. This darkened shadow is a sight that opens up in this dim light to show me hands that reach for me. I'm so afraid I cannot speak. I cannot breath. I cannot move. I cannot run. I need help. No one is there. I try to pray, but it is despair. Who do I call? Who do I turn to? I mumble words that have no meaning, only sounds that keep me dreaming. I close my eyes and dare not look. I hold on for my dear life. I cannot bear this mental strife. I float down and see this angel's gown cover me in a sheet of white as I stand there in the night.

On this clear and moonlit night, as I quietly ponder, my thoughts far and distant search mysterious times and places. I'm drawn by silent laughter and the melody of song. Creatures far and yet quite near outside and then inside the graves sing a catchy eerie tune. I recall it was November on the day of all the souls, and the light from burning torches cast shadows on the tombs. Swaying movements stopped my thinking as I glanced some dancing shapes. First one and then another coming close as one departs, leaving the first in dire mourning and heartfelt wrenching sorrow. As I stood carefully watching, I could feel a presence there. I could hear a solemn tune a couple long ago held dear. How could I describe it and put it down in words? It was soft like a feather. It enraptured like a dream. It enchanted like a star. It was here and then afar. A violin was playing as I tried to concentrate. The chords kept interrupting, and they seemed to penetrate. My mind blocked it out, but the haunting sound was magic. It was a spell that took my senses. Mesmerized, I looked and jumped back in sudden fright. She was standing there beside me, beckoning as she placed her hand on mine, and on her cheek was a tear. I held her, and we danced as I recognized the tune. We moved to the music. I kept up with every step. She was beautiful and warm, pleasant and endearing. Her eyes gazed on mine, and I was under her spell. As we danced, I held her tight. Then, without a thought, I embraced her. I closed my eyes and felt her cheek. I touched her hair and caressed her. Then I reached down to kiss her hungry blood red lips, and she melted in my arms. Then slowly, very slowly, she faded away, slipping back into dark shadows.

Apparitions whisper rumors. Unexplained melodies I hear that further my inner fear. Haunting verses capture me as I strain my eyes in vain to see. The ominous air enshrouds the tombstones as I try to unravel this mystery. Dark specters plague my being from these shivering graveyards that I'm seeing. Misty figures emerge when I listen to a dirge. Then Bibiana casts a shadow as

"The Graves," photograph by Santiago de Aragón, 2013. *Courtesy of the author.*

she continues to roam in these hair-raising haunts. And she chillingly taunts, "Come to me, I beg you come to me." Briskly she follows me, never escaping her she chases. Oh, what fear to see her, what fright, what horror! Looking like an angel of death, a monster in the dark, a vampire that appears, dying from hunger and thirst. Although I yell and then I run, she is always, always present. Was this an illusion, my weakness, or my human darkness? Was it a ghost, a phantasm, my dementia and nothing more? I'm left with a bizarre fear of the unknown. I'm left with insecurity and the thought of what comes after we depart? At the end of the road, there's crying and fear. At the end of the road, all grief is held dear. Sorrows end, anguish, suffering, lost loves, and everything one feels. Memories are left, things to remember, grudges, curses, and all we recall. A wooden cross remains as a sign, and a handful of dirt is all that is mine. In the gloom of this night, as I stand quietly praying, winged demons threaten my soul with all of their might. In the stillness of the night, hideous creatures watch me to see if I stray from what is right. In livid darkness of the night, gruesome screams abound as I turn and look and try to be contrite. Coffins creak, tombs open, undead rise, evil lurks in foreboding places in this gloom of the night.

Come to me, she pleads. Come to me, she begs. Come to me. She goes on, "In the night, they hear me crying, crying for you. Between tears and anguish, I feel your love. I am forsaken. Like a thief, you stole my heart and mortal body. You owe me. Give me my life once again. Please, please help me to begin." I ask what she is saying. Is she confused? Someone she loved and was refused. And yet she feels me, and I feel her. Deep within me, something changes as it were. In my soul, I'm filled with fear, a thing of darkness so unclear. It pulls within me till I yearn to bring that memory back again. All I know is that this night, I heard her hideous crying, crying. I searched it out because of caring, caring for this one in pain. I found Bibiana in the blackness, reaching out to me in sadness. Such a horrid sight I see. Her face was blotched with greenish shadows, purple lines and graying skin like someone from deep within the grave. She touched me with her mournful story. A tale full of love and sorrow. And yet each day and passing moment, it brings her another dreary night. This Bibiana is a spirit, wandering in an endless search. Her mournful crying is always blowing, blowing through the dark foreboding paths. No one knows just how to help her, how to place her heart at peace. Her soul is in such dire torment. She only wants her pain to cease. She is always pleading, always begging for a key that will break open and end all her suffering. Bibiana is immortal, tied down to this earth. She had a birth but yet no end. She tends to the Book of the Living Dead. Sadly, my name is inscribed on its yellowed pages.

María Sangre Fría— Bloody Mary

Stories are told that María Flores lived in El Porvenir, a ghost town in northeastern New Mexico. People believed that El Porvenir, located in a beautiful setting with pools of crisp, clear water; grassy fields; and nearby hills filled with towering pine trees, was a perfect place to build a future. A little church was erected to hold *santos*, the wonderfully carved religious images adored on saints' feast days and other special occasions. Farms were established, and people planned a store to market their fruit and vegetables. In 1898, the Flores family, an older couple with a little girl, and their parrot, Chucho, moved in. No one knew where the family came from.

María Flores was about nine years old. She had long jet-black hair and bright steel-gray eyes. She was very neatly dressed. Her elderly companions hobbled along with canes. The trio settled into a small adobe house near a stream at the edge of town. María and Chucho liked to play outside, but she was a very strange child. She enjoyed talking to her parrot but disliked being around people, especially other children. One bright and sunny day, Maria saw a couple of the town girls walking up a path between the trees. She quietly tiptoed behind a boulder and fired her slingshot. She hit one of the girls smack dab on the forehead. They both ran off screaming as the blood gushed out of the poor girl's head. Of course, no one knew who had done it.

The elderly couple spoiled María Flores rotten. They gave her everything she wanted. Pretty dresses, special foods—María got anything her little heart desired. The old man and woman showered the overindulged girl with endless attention. They lived only for her. A question circulated

"Girl with Parrot," cabinet card by T.J. Curran, circa 1890. *Courtesy of the author.*

around El Porvenir. People wanted to know what the relationship was between María and the old couple. Were they her grandparents? No one knew, but everyone wondered.

The couple made it very clear that no one was welcome on their land. At times, the people from the village would purposely pass by to see what the old man spent his time doing in his front yard. They were especially curious because old man Flores spent a lot of his time whittling strange figures out of wood. He would go into the forest in search of special wood. The figures he carved were writhing grotesque figures with wide eyes and gaping mouths. The carver would sing peculiar songs and talk to himself in a foreign tongue. Occasionally, Chucho would also join in the singing. He, too, knew the strange language of his possessors. Sometimes the old man would even cradle his figures, chant some words and then get up and do a funny dance with them. His carvings seemed to have a life of their own after the old man's ritual.

The old woman spent much of her time going into the hills to dig up roots and pick leaves from certain plants. She also had an herb garden, but it wasn't a typical herb garden. The plants themselves were quite unusual. They were more like odd weeds with a terrible odor. She also would chant while tending her plants. Sometimes she would pick at a leaf, break it in half and then take in a deep breath as she held it to her wiggling nose. That would have made most of us choke and throw up. Indeed, they were a very strange family.

María Flores, which means Mary Flowers in English, was a cold and distant child. Whenever the unusual trio was walking in town, she would glare at everyone, especially other children her own age. They wanted to taunt her. But she would sneer at them, and they were too scared. In secret, the little boys would say, "She is rotten, made out of cotton." Chucho would cry out, "She's gonna get you…gonna get you…gonna get you." Then they would run off. María would turn and look back and give a smile that would send shivers up and down their little spines. How did she and her bird know what they were thinking? Did she sense their fear? Yes, she was different—not at all like anyone they had ever met before. And her bird seemed to contribute to this mystery.

Every boy and girl in El Porvenir knew that there were certain rules to follow. For instance, if you lost a tooth, you would have to go out of the house at midday, close your eyes and throw it with all of your might toward the sun. You also had to collect your fingernails when you cut them and burn them in the fire of a wood-burning stove. Cut hair required special attention.

Girls could donate it to a *santero*, a maker of holy images, for use on statues meant for churches or chapels. Boys had to bury theirs. This was a tradition hundreds of years old. If a witch ever discovered their discarded teeth, nails or hair, she would certainly use it in evil potions against them.

María Flores wasn't concerned about evil witches. She didn't fear anything. She collected her baby teeth, cut finger and toenails and saved locks of her hair in defiance of all the old wives' tales. She hid everything in a silver chest she kept under her bed. She learned from her guardians to hide her precious things. They encouraged her to follow their example. One never knew when these things would be useful. These and other strange habits caused horrible gossip to circulate in town. These Flores people were certainly up to no good and were harmful to the good name and reputation of the community.

One day, when the old woodcarver was very busy whittling away, María went up to him and said, "I want a doll." He answered, "*Sí, hijita, lo que tu quieras*" (Yes, whatever you want my child). The old man instructed the little girl to go into the forest and search for the wood she wanted. Chucho did not wish to join her on this adventure. She left right away. Not finding what she was looking for, she went deeper and deeper into the forest. After several hours of crossing streams, jumping rocks, tripping and falling, she was ready to give up hope. Just then, María saw an enormous wrangled tree trunk, and when she looked up, arm-like branches spread out as far as the eyes could see. "I want one of these branches," she thought.

María Flores attempted to climb up the tree, but she fell off each time. The more she fell, the more determined she became. It was hopeless. The tree was too big and the branches too high. Dejected, she looked down and cried. Just then, a branch came crashing down and landed right in front of her feet. María jumped for joy, but she hadn't noticed that when the branch fell, she got a cut on her head. She was too excited to care if the blood from the wound ran down her face, went into her eyes, down her arms and onto the hungry branch, which soaked it all up. She was a bloody mess. Happily, she pulled the bloody dead branch all the way home.

Upon reaching home, Chucho began to cry out, "Bloody Mary, Bloody Mary, Bloody Mary." The old woman rushed out to meet María. She immediately began cleaning her child, and the woodcarver put his loving fingers to work on creating a beautiful doll for María. After a few days, the doll was complete and ready for the old woman to make a beautiful dress for it from one of the little girl's old dresses. María wanted to use her own black hair, so they made a wig and glued it on. She took out her silver chest and also glued on some of her finger and toenails into place on the doll.

"Girl with Doll," Carte-de-Visite, unknown photographer, circa 1885. *Courtesy of the author.*

The old man carved tiny sockets underneath the lips and proudly smiled as María very carefully placed her baby teeth into the doll's mouth. It was a perfect fit. The happy girl named her doll Ari, which is a nickname for María. She cuddled it, slept with it and talked to her doll deep into each dark night. During trips into town, María carried her doll under her arm, and her parrot clung to her shoulder. Chucho had gotten into the practice of calling the doll Bloody Mary over and over again. The children laughed and repeated what the parrot said.

Sadly, it turned out that María Flores became very sick one cold winter. She had insisted on playing outside without putting on a coat. She was tough. She was strong. The cold wouldn't hurt her, she said to her loving guardians as she ran out of the house. The wind was howling outside the house, and the snow blanketed the ground. No matter what the old woman did with her magical herb teas and roots, María's illness grew worse. But a strange thing began to happen. The more pale and weak Maria got, the more alive the doll became. The colder María's body felt, the warmer the doll became. While she held on to her doll, María died. The parrot left home and never returned. The old man and woman were heartbroken. They took María's frail body to the town photographer to have a memento mori, or mourning picture, taken of her before her burial. The photo was of her and her doll. They were both dressed the same with pretty red bows in their hair, new socks and new shoes. The old woman, covered from head to toe in a long black shawl, held María and her doll on her lap. The image revealed a lifeless little girl and a smiling doll. The elderly couple decided to keep the doll and not bury it with María.

The old man lost interest in carving, and the old woman sat in her rocking chair all day with the doll in her arms. They never did anything anymore. They mourned María Flores so much that eventually they couldn't bear to even look at the doll. One day, the old woman took the doll and carefully placed her in María's silver box. Ari's face no longer had a smile. Soon after this, on a windy and stormy morning, the couple didn't wake up. The old man and the old woman had died in their sleep during the night. The people spread all kinds of rumors about why they were never seen, and they also talked about strange red arm-like old tree branches that covered the outside of the house. The bloody branches seemed to increase as the months passed. Eventually, they began to wonder if someone should visit the small adobe house. After all, the couple was very old. No one volunteered. They were afraid of the consequences since the old couple never allowed anyone on their property. The townspeople were always suspicious and wondered if they practiced witchcraft. Everyone kept away from the couple's house because of fear.

One day, Valeria Valdez, a little girl about the age of María Flores, and three of her friends got the courage and went to María's home. The doors and windows were blocked by the bizarre red branches, which embraced the house and seemed to come from the inside, since they were not part of any tree on the outside. The inexplicable movement of the branches caused Valeria's friends to scream and run back into town. They called for Valeria, but she would not come. Like María Flores, she was not fearful of anything. Valeria found an opening between the bloody branches big enough for her to squeeze through. When she entered the house, she was shocked to find that the branches were everywhere. Valeria made her way through the house and finally came to a room with a bed and two skeletons lying on it. She noticed that the branches seemed to start at the bed, which held the skeletons in place.

Valeria looked under the bed and noticed there was a silver box. As she reached for the box, the branches retracted. For a moment, the young girl hesitated with fear, since she had cut her arms somehow. But then she took the box. Her heart raced as she opened the silver chest. When she opened it, she found María's smiling doll, which exposed its tiny teeth. The doll's eyes were closed. What an unexpected surprise. The doll was quite beautiful. Valeria took the silver chest with the doll inside and found her way out of the house. Upon reaching her home, she took the chest and hid it in her bedroom closet. Exhausted, Valeria's parents walked in. "Where were you?" they cried. "Why are you covered in blood? Your friends said you had not returned with them and thought you had been taken into the old couple's house. Some of the men cut enough branches off the entrance of the door to rescue you from inside but only found two skeletons lying on a bed." Valeria's father picked her up and took her into the bathroom so that her mother could wash her off. "Did someone hurt you?" her father asked. Valeria smiled and said she wasn't hurt and didn't know where the blood had come from. Her parents scolded her and told her she was never to go to that house again. The village was making arrangements to have the old couple buried, and the house burned down to the ground. There was something very wicked about the bloody branches that covered it.

One dark and dreary night, Valeria took the doll out of the chest to play with it. She was frightened when she heard a noise at her window. Valeria opened the window to see where the noise was coming from. Suddenly, Chucho flew into the room and made himself at home. Valeria found herself attached to the parrot as if he had always been hers. She never told anyone that she had actually entered the house, nor did she tell them about what she had found. Every time she had some time to herself, she would take the doll out of its silver coffin and play with it. Chucho would automatically call out, "Bloody Mary, Bloody Mary, Bloody Mary!" But then something very strange happened one night. Valeria had moved her chair to a different part of the room. When she looked up, she saw that she was sitting in front of the large mirror hanging in her room. The reflection in the mirror was that of a bloodstained doll. She looked at the doll on her lap, and it looked as it always had. But in the mirror, it was covered in blood. She thought of putting it into the fire and burning it. Chucho screamed, "Bloody Mary, Bloody Mary, Bloody Mary!" She thought again, stood up and walked up to the mirror. The reflection in the mirror was of Bloody Mary, and holding her was María Flores.

The doll's eyes, which had remained closed since she found it, began to slowly open. Valeria at first thought it was her imagination, but then the doll's arms and hands began to move as she held it. The mouth moved, and Valeria knew she heard it call out, "Ma-rí-a-a-a." The poor girl was petrified. Valeria moved her eyes away from the doll and tried to push it away from her. The harder she pulled the doll away from her, the tighter the grip became. Valeria tried to move out of her bedroom, but suddenly the door was covered with bloody branch limbs. She furiously pulled at the door, but it wouldn't open. Valeria could hardly breathe because the doll was holding tightly around her neck. As she moved backward, she fell onto her bed. Immediately, bloody branches held her in place. She could not move. She could not breathe. Saddened, by the loss of another friend, Bloody Mary returned to her silver box, waiting for the day when someone would find her and love her as much as María Flores.

They say Valeria Valdez died from shock. They also say, "Left for love and good for spite; left or right, good at night. What do you see and what do you hear? The day has eyes, and the night has ears."

Knock, Knock, Who's There?

Es fácil ver pero difícil prever.
It's easy to see but hard to foresee.

It was the Lenten season, the time of the solemn rituals of the Passion sufferings of Jesus Christ during his trial, crucifixion and burial. Everyone in the town of Peñasco Blanco, White Rock, was preparing for this annual folk commemoration, celebrated since medieval times. The Hermanos de la Sangre, Brothers of Blood, and Los Hermanos de las Tinieblas, the Brothers of Darkness, slowly made their way late at night down a rock-strewn trail covered with thistles, cactus and jagged stones. These members of the Penitente Brotherhood wore black masks and white cotton drawers, were shirtless and walked barefoot. They whipped their backs with yucca fibrous braided cords, just as their ancestors had done for centuries before them. The flagellants were led by the Hermanos de la Luz, the Brothers of Light, who carried lanterns to light the way; recited prayers called *alabados*; whirled *matracas*, which were wood rattles; played flutes; and did drum rolls. These leaders of the lay confraternity sang doleful hymns drawn from *cuadernos*. These small memorandum books were filled with sorrowful chants and memories about the sorrows of Mary and her divine son.

As the group of Penitentes agonizingly reached the village of adobe, mud-bricked and mud-plastered houses, it was a scene to behold. Curious children peeked out of windows as adults told them to pray. The intermittent thuds of the whips could be heard. The lanterns invading the night created shadows

"Penitente Morada de San Juan Nepomuceno," real photo postcard, unknown photographer and date. *Courtesy of the author.*

that looked like mysterious specters from another time. The children called the figures "Espíritos Dolientes," Ghostly Spirits, even though this group was made up of their fathers, grandfathers and uncles and other male members of the community. The sad and mournful hymns that were sung echoed throughout the valley. The young boys knew that someday, it would be their turn to belong to this order. It was a rite of passage that was cherished and recognized from one generation to another. They would have to memorize the ancient alabados. They had to make their own copy of the book and carry it for the remainder of their lives once they were full-fledged members of this Catholic group of Spanish men who stemmed from the early saints of the church.

Pablita Sánchez, Eloisa Romero and other women in Peñasco Blanco belonged to Las Hermanas de la Santísima Cruz, the Sisters of the Holy Cross. It was their duty to cut and sew clothing for the *santos*, the holy wooden images of Christ, Mary and the saints at the church and the Penitente *morada*. The morada, located in a hidden area of the mountains, was the meetinghouse and ceremonial center for the men. The women had their own secluded morada, where they held their own services and whipped their backs in atonement for their sins, as their Spanish women forbears had done for centuries. Among the popular images were statues of the Ecce Homo (the Man of Sorrows), crucifixes and Doña Sebastiana, variously called the Venerable Lady, La Huesuda, Bone Lady or simply La Muerte (Death). This frightening carved image of the Angel of Death reminded everyone that death is ever present. One never knows when she will appear and take you, so you have to be ready. Sitting in her "Death Cart" with a drawn bow and arrow, this dark angel is always prepared to strike. She has no favorites. Rich and poor alike are all within her grasp.

The women penitents also made hand-stitched altar cloths and other decorations for the churches and moradas. They were quite expert at the fiber arts, such as making embroidered pieces and quilts. This was a tradition passed down from mother to daughter since the early Spanish settlement of New Mexico in the sixteenth century. The little girls of the village had their own rite of passage. There was a group called Las Veronicas. The story goes that a woman named Veronica encountered Christ as he traveled on La Via Dolorosa, his sorrowful journey to the crucifixion. He was bloodied, beaten and scourged. Veronica felt deep and extreme pain in her heart when she saw him. She removed a cloth that covered her head and very tenderly wiped the tears of blood and sweat from Christ's face. His Rostro Santo, divine face, was miraculously imprinted on the cloth. Later in life, Veronica traveled to Rome, where she presented the cloth with the image to the Hispano-Roman emperor Tiberius, who was deathly ill. He was immediately cured. When Veronica died, she left the cloth, now called the Sudarium, to Pope Saint Clement. Word spread that the Sudarium had magical powers that could cure blindness and even raise the dead.

In Spanish colonial New Mexico, young girls emulated Santa Veronica. They had to be chaste and very pious. The Veronicas meditated on the life of Jesus and, of course, his mother, Mary, who was central to their faith. Little girls in Peñasco Blanco could not cut their hair. When it was long and it measured below their waists, one of the girls was selected as a Veronica. This meant that her hair could be cut and used to fashion a wig for one of the holy images. All of the girls who had been awarded this distinction each year then belonged to the Veronicas. Then, as young women, they could move on to become Sisters of the Holy Cross. These girls made their own copybooks of religious hymns. Both the girls and the boys were taught how to read and write by the female family members in the villages, so literacy was extremely high in New Mexico.

The elderly female penitents held the distinction of providing their long, braided white hair for the grisly death figures. The hair had to be as white as snow. They also made black dresses for these skeleton statues and placed long black shawls on the skulls with hollow eye sockets similar to the shawls called *rebozos* or *tapalos*, which they wore. Some *muertes*, death figures, were doll sized and carried in procession. Both men and women participated in a community Passion play wherein they reenacted the scenes of the final days of Christ. A particularly beautiful reenactment was El Encuentro, the encounter between Mary and her son. In this scene, the women carried La Dolorosa, a statue representing Mary as Our Lady of Sorrows, and the men carried El Jesús Nazareno, a statue of the thorn-crowned Christ with wounds covering his body. In a very touching ceremony, both statues meet in a heartrending scene that is recalled in verse.

Pablita Sánchez and her husband, Filimón, had twelve children—six boys and six girls. Families in New Mexico were quite large in those days. It was the 1930s, the time of the Great Depression. Many people were out of work and had to endure numerous hardships, including starvation. The Depression wasn't felt as much in Peñasco Blanco because people farmed and raised livestock. They didn't need money. They also had fruit trees and vegetables on the fertile land. The women canned and also dried fruit. They produced strips of dried beef called *carne seca*. The women prepared the delicious Lenten meals of Torta de Huevo, which are meringued and seasoned deep-fried eggs smothered in red chile. They also made *quelites*, a dish of spinach sautéed with onions, and pinto beans seasoned with dried red chile flakes and salt. They prepared different meals that their Penitente husbands and sons could take with them when they spent days away from home at the morada. Once home after Lent was over, Pablita's sons helped their father tending the sheep, pigs and cattle and mending fences. Her young daughters helped her head up into the hills to dig up the roots of the amole plant to make shampoo. They also searched out brush plants to make brooms. Back at home, they churned butter and made bar soap out of pigs' fat, as well as candles and a variety of cheeses. The boys and men worked from sunup to sundown. Women's work never ceased. Life was hard, but people were happy.

On Good Friday, the sorrow-filled day remembered as Christ's crucifixion, Pablita and her daughters rushed to get ready. They would be attending a supernatural Tenebrae Service called Las Tinieblas at the men's morada. This ritual had roots in the early Christian church. Filimón Sánchez was an Hermano Mayor, an elder brother who was in charge of the service. He wanted to be sure his wife and younger children would be on time. The service began later in the evening. The *tenebrario*, a triangular candlestick holding fifteen candles, was lit when everyone settled in and sat on the hard dirt floor. During this Service of the Shadows for Holy Week, solemn Stations of the Cross, or the Vía Cruces, retold the emotional story of the

The Undead

"Instruments of Tinieblas," photograph by Rosa María Calles. © *Rosa María Calles*.

"New Mexico Adobe," postcard by J.R. Willis, unknown date. *Courtesy of the author*.

Passion of Christ. After each station, a candle was extinguished until the last candle on top, which represented the light of Christ, was removed and hidden at midnight. The morada was then plunged into total darkness. Suddenly, pandemonium broke loose. This was signaled with stomping on the dirt floor. The convulsion of nature with earthquakes, rocks splitting and the dead rising from their graves was expressed with thunderous noise. Everyone chanted, "*Salgan, salgan, salgan almas*" (Leave, leave, leave souls) as they furiously beat on pots and pans and whirled *matracas*, ratcheted noisemakers. Anything that could make a loud noise, such as washboards, chains, flutes and drums, were heard. The Brothers of Blood groaned in the dark. Finally, the lit candle showing the light of Christ was returned. This signaled the end of lamentations, and people quietly returned home. After Holy Week, things got back to normal in Peñasco Blanco.

One day, Pablita was cooking in the kitchen. She had pots of pinto beans and red chile with pork simmering on the woodstove. She was also making tortillas and baking an apple pie. It was a glorious smell. Her friend Eloisa dropped in for a visit and pulled up a chair. Pablita handed her a cup of coffee and some freshly baked *pastelitos*, miniature fruit-filled pies. Both of them were *comadriando*, sharing stories, as usual. Without warning, Eloisa exclaimed, "Pablita, you and I have been close friends for a very long time." "Yes we have been," Pablita answered. Eloisa continued, "You know we're both getting older." Pablita turned around from the stove and noticed that her friend had a very serious look on her face. "*Qué te pasa?* What's wrong?" she asked. Eloisa responded, "You know we're both getting older, and someday we're going to die!" "Well everyone has to die sooner or later," Pablita responded. "I know, I know, but I've been giving this a lot of thought lately. I think we should make each other a promise." Pablita, wanting to reassure her troubled friend and put her mind at ease, quickly nodded her head in agreement, adding, "Sí, sí, we'll make a promise." Eloisa got a grim look on her face. "I'm not joking. I'm being serious. I think we should make a promise to each other that if you die before me, you will let me know, and if I die before you, I will let you know." Pablita was surprised with her friend's strange request. After thinking seriously for a moment, she told her, "Bueno, okay. If I die first, I will let you know, and if you go before me, let me know." Eloisa's sad look immediately changed. "It's a promise then," she cried out. She got up from the chair and gave her friend a hug. Pablita never gave it a second thought.

Days, months and even years passed by. Filimón opened a store in the nearby town of Mora. It was located on the main street. At his store, he

Pensamientos (Thoughts), nineteenth-century engraving, unknown engraver. *Courtesy of the author.*

sold potatoes, freshly butchered meat and other staples. Pablita always had dinner ready and set on the table when Filimón got back from town. The children had to wait to eat until their father arrived. One evening, they all waited and waited, but Filimón did not return at his usual time. This was very unusual for Filimón. Pablita started to worry. "Children, eat and get ready for bed. We will pray for his safe return until he gets home. I hope nothing has happened to your father," she said. It was already dark when they finally heard a noise outside the door. *"Oh, gracias a Dios,* thanks to God, your father is home!" They all heard footsteps outside and a knock on the door, and then the doorknob started turning. A minute later, they heard another dull knock on the door. Pablita always kept the door locked for safety since the house was isolated. She also knew her husband carried his key with him. After a third knock, the doorknob turned again, but this time the door slowly opened. Pablita's youngest daughters, who were six and seven years old, quickly hid under their mother's long skirt and peeked out toward the door. The old wooden door then completely opened. Only darkness could be seen outside. Pablita was frightened, but she had to protect her children, so she got the courage to rush up to the door and slam it shut. A second later, more noise was heard outside. A horse-drawn wagon could be heard, as could footsteps. These were hurried steps. The doorknob turned, but this time the door didn't open. A key was heard sliding into the keyhole, and Filimón walked in. He walked right up to Pablita and said, "I was already near home when I passed by José and Eloisa's house. José came running out and stopped me. He said he needed my help. I got down and went inside with him. Eloisa was in the bedroom lying on the bed. José said she slipped and hit her head. The pillowcase was covered in blood. We did everything we could, but we couldn't save her! Pablita, Eloisa died." Pablita burst into tears. She told Filimón what had occurred earlier and about the promise Eloisa and she had made. Pablita then knew her dear friend had kept her promise.

In the Gloom of the Night

The boards on the open porch creaked as Julio stepped onto them. His steps were slow and deliberate. The young man hesitated for a moment before knocking on the door. He had thoughts of backing out and forgetting the whole thing. Too late—the door was opening before he had a chance to turn around and walk away. "I thought I heard footsteps outside," a woman said with a strong voice. This woman was well known in the community of Socorro. Her name was Sidelia. She was an *adivinadora*. This was someone who could foresee the future. Sidelia didn't have a crystal ball or Tarot cards, and she couldn't read tea leaves. She had a supernatural gift that was hard to explain. She could look into your eyes and read your mind. She was scary, but people respected and trusted her because she could help them with their troubles. "So you have trouble sleeping?" she asked Julio. He was dumbfounded not only by her question but also by her looks. Sidelia was a small woman, less than five feet tall. She had a medium build and was very white-skinned with long white hair that she wore in a bun. A *tapalina*, a short bonnet, covered her hair. Even though Sidelia was short, she was a striking figure of a woman. She was assertive and self-assured. Her brilliant blue eyes sparkled like stars. Her face broke into a broad smile when he saw her. She invited him inside, and he was stunned by what he smelled and saw.

A strong odor permeated the entire room. A dog ran into the room and began growling and snapping at Julio. "Oh Pancha, behave! She won't bite you," said Sidelia. "She just doesn't like strangers. I have another pet around here somewhere. His name is Coco. He is one of my newer pets. I had another dog, but a car hit him last week. I was heartbroken by my loss. I was so lonely without Spook that I got my Coco. His owner finally sold him to me for $100. Here is his certificate hanging on the wall. Registered dogs are pretty expensive, aren't they? I usually take in stray dogs and cats. They have a good home here. Would you like to see my little monkey? She's pregnant, though she has had a lot of complications. The poor little thing is so tired all the time." Julio never got a word in since she never waited long enough for an answer.

Julio was led into another room, where he saw a collection of every object and animal imaginable. He checked the floor, ceiling and walls expecting to see something crawl out. He viewed everything with a suspicious eye. A snake slithered along the floor, searching for something to eat. Then a loud piercing sound caught his attention. His wide eyes turned, searched and questioned. Sidelia noticed, and she quickly said proudly, "Don't be afraid. It's just my pig, Gariblanco. It's getting cold outside, so I brought Gariblanco inside. Look at him here in the corner. He's getting nice and fat. Oh, I can tell you don't like pigs. Let's go into my kitchen to talk." They both walked into the kitchen, where she pumped water from a well into the sink and filled a teapot. She had Julio sit down at the table and a few minutes later served him a cup of hot mint tea. "This will help you to relax. I'm having some, too." She joined him at the table.

"I moved here because I like the name Socorro," she said. "Do you know that *socorro* means 'help'?" Julio just listened without saying a word. He couldn't if he had wanted to because she never stopped talking. She went from one subject to another, apparently not caring for any response.

> *Many years ago, some of our Spanish ancestors who had settled here were attacked by a band of Indians. The situation was hopeless. It turned out that some presidio soldiers who were out patrolling were passing nearby. The settlers yelled, "Socorro!" as loud as they could. The brave soldiers heard their screams for help, so they rushed over to help them and killed many of the Indians. Some of the Indian warriors had made off with a couple of the girls, but the soldiers were able to rescue the girls. A church was built, and it was dedicated to Nuestra Señora del Socorro, Our Lady of Assistance. Enough chitchat! I'm here to assist you. How can I help you? You're having bad dreams, aren't you?*

"How can you tell?" Julio asked. "Your eyes are red. You look tired, and you look like someone who hasn't slept well," she answered. "I've been having these nightmares," said Julio. "I had a twin brother who died a few months ago..." "Tell me about him," Sidelia interjected.

> *Alfonso, my brother, always walked in his sleep. I always had to be looking out for him. I was always in charge of him ever since we were little boys. My mother would tell me to make sure he wouldn't get hurt. He would try climbing trees and would fall down. He would get into the ditches when they were full of water and would almost drown. Alfonso was always doing stupid things. We don't know how he wound up getting into the pigs' corral. The only thing we could tell was that he must have been trying to feed the pigs. The corral is high up, and we have to use a ladder when we give them food. It was pretty cold, and it had snowed. There was ice on the fence and posts. He must have slipped, fell in and hit his head. The pigs attacked him. It was awful. My father and I hit the pigs with boards to try getting them away from his body, but they didn't move. Finally, my father shot them with his rifle. My mother blamed me for everything because I wasn't there to help him, as she had ordered me to do. She hasn't been the same since then. Now I have bad dreams every night, and they won't go away. I keep seeing Alfonso over and over again. Sometimes we're children in my dreams. I'm chasing him, asking him to be careful as we play. Other times I dream we're happy and having fun and then suddenly he is in a black coffin. My mother is right. I'm to blame for what happened to Alfonso. I should have been there for him.*

Sidelia could see Julio was setting himself up for a breakdown and wouldn't be able to sort out his feelings, so she started to ramble again:

> *Oh yes, pigs can be very dangerous. But in our culture, we do love our pork. We can't live without* chicharones. *I just love those fried pork cracklings with tortillas. I'm getting hungry just thinking about it. Do you know we got flour tortillas from the Arabs? Not pork! They don't eat pork! Can you believe that? Come to think of it, we got a lot from the Arabs. Our Spanish language has many Arabic words, like* moreno, morena, mora. *Have you been to Mora? I love that little town. Just think, some pigs can weigh several hundred pounds when they are ready for the* matanza. *People are always inviting me to the slaughter and cooking of a pig. If you like a good party, you have to go to a matanza, where there is plenty to eat for everyone and everything is so delicious.*

Wallow in Mire, block print from *The English Usurer* by John Blaxton, London, 1634. *Courtesy of the author.*

Julio couldn't believe what he was hearing. He felt like he was having a nervous breakdown. He had just told her about his dead brother and his mother, who now hated him, and she was giving him a history lesson! "What was I thinking in coming here?" Julio thought. "Why did I think she could help me? She's crazy!" His face took on a look of anger as he got up from his chair and started to walk away. Sidelia quickly held him back and apologized for being so insensitive. "I'm sorry, hijito," she said. "I know you're upset, and I go on and on. But I'm not crazy. There's a reason for my madness." Julio stopped. "Come, sit down," Sidelia pleaded. He did as he was told.

Sidelia began talking in a more reasonable tone. "Julio, it isn't your fault. You did the best you could. You couldn't be with him every minute of the day. Your mother is grieving, and when you lose someone you love, you want to find others to blame." Julio cut in: "I fed the pigs every day, and Alfonso was always with me. When he called out that he was going to feed the pigs ahead of me, I should have gotten out of bed immediately. But I was cold and lazy. If I had gotten there sooner, I could have stopped him!" Sidelia explained:

Few people realize that pigs can be very aggressive when they feel threatened. They won't hesitate to attack you. Pigs have sharp teeth that can eat through anything. They are also very unpredictable. You don't know what they're going to do. Alfonso wasn't the first to be killed by pigs, and he won't be the last. Pigs can kill people. There are many horror stories I could tell you of people killed by pigs because they were careless. Not all pigs are like this, but some will even attack other animals. You have to start them as newborns if you want to have them as pets. They are often kept in small fenced-up areas where they don't have room to move around. I guess I could get mean under those conditions. But you know, if you think about it, dogs are our best friends and they can kill you.

Julio was calm now.

Sidelia got up and served Julio another cup of tea. Then, strangely, she began talking to herself. Julio couldn't understand what she was saying. Suddenly, she said, "I feel a presence in this room along with you. It's a good presence. It isn't anything to be afraid of. Sometimes we have the ability to communicate with the dead. I think that is what is happening here. I know you feel a lot of guilt for your brother's death and you want me to foretell your future. Well I can tell you…" Just then, Sidelia's monkey appeared and jumped onto the table. "Oh there you are, Pifania. What have you been up to? Say hello to our new friend. His name is Julio. He's here so we can help him." The adivinadora cradled the monkey in her arms. "Julio, this is what you have to do," Sidelia continued. "Get yourself a statue of Our Lady of Socorro and light a candle to her every night. Reflect on the good memories of your brother and move on. Your mother and father will eventually be happy and be very proud of what you achieve in life. Dedicate your achievements to Alfonso. Julio, you have a life worth living. Alfonso is in a better place. I know he is happy, and he is also concerned about you. He worries about you. His spirit is with you." She continued, "God helps those who help themselves. Go out and help yourself."

Julio actually felt relieved when he left Sidelia's house. He began attending church and prayed every day. He didn't get over the nightmares right away. It took a little time, but each day, Julio and his parents got better and began to enjoy life once again. He also helped others when they needed socorro. Julio knew that socorro meant "help," and helping others was his calling in life. He became a priest.

La Muerte Pays a Visit

For New Mexicans, money was not as much of a treasure as rain. The rain was important to everyone's livelihood. Water fed the crops, which, in turn, brought happiness and security to the people. It made the land green, with an abundance of color coming from the vegetables, fruit and beautiful flowers that covered the space across the descending hills, woodlands and even the *llanos*, the plains, that spread throughout New Mexico. Droughts brought hardship to the people with a lack of food for themselves and their animals. An ancient tradition was renewed after the pastures close to the settlements were depleted and sheep owners had to hire sheepherders to tend to their flocks in the wide-open llanos. Life in the llanos was lonely, difficult and, oftentimes, very dangerous.

Sheepherding became the leading industry of New Mexico and, for many, was the only type of employment they could find up to the time of the WPA in the 1930s. The Work Projects Administration was a program started by the government under President Franklin Delano Roosevelt in 1939 to provide employment for those who were out of work. Hispanos who owned the large herds of sheep prospered. A *partida* usually consisted of one thousand head of sheep. There were also the *caporales*, men who were hired to visit the camps with supplies for the sheepherders and replenish their drinking water. Sheepherders spent all their time with the sheep and were too far away from places that could provide what they needed. Many traditions came from this isolated style of living. Some of the sheepherders were musicians, poets and storytellers. When the camps were close enough

The Stock, engraving by Henry Winkles, circa 1880. *Author's collection.*

to one another, the sheepherders came together in the evenings to sing and tell stories of their adventures. Many *corridos*, or ballads, were written about their experiences, which also served as a documentation of the life of the sheepherder.

This was the setting that would influence a religious sheepherder by the name of Roman Jaramillo at a very young age and for the rest of his life. Roman, the son of Elijio and Felicitas Jaramillo, was born in 1908. Elijio had also been a sheepherder. Before Roman celebrated his thirteenth birthday, his father passed away. Felicitas supported her family by planting a garden, which served to feed her family and produce vegetables for trade. She also was paid for washing clothes for other families and sewing wedding dresses for women of the community. Roman missed his family when he was out sheepherding, so he would come home after three months and take at least a month before returning. It was a lonely life, especially when other sheepherders' camps were so far away from one another that they couldn't gather at night. Roman watched his flock by day, traveling many miles while the sheep grazed on the range. During the time of little rain, it was important to also find a spring or natural water source. Of course, if there had been rain, the sheepherder could find many springs gushing from the earth in the llano. At night, Roman moved his flock to camp, where he prepared his food and where he slept. He did not like going in the winter, when sheepherding was harder than during other times of the year. If it was cold, the herders built fires around the herds. The fires were kept burning day and night. Each year in the summer, shearers went from camp to camp. The sheepherder would catch up to what was happening in the towns and farms away from the llano when the shearers were around.

On one of Roman's trips home, he was told it was time to marry, and a wife was chosen for him. At the age of eighteen, he was married to Candelaria, the daughter of Doña Ramona Gallegos, who was a widow. He went out in search of another type of work because he did not want to leave his family for such a long time, as was required when sheepherding. Roman purchased a *carro de caballos*, a horse-drawn wagon, with big red wheels. Roman and his young wife traveled throughout New Mexico and would make camp in their wagon along the side of the road. They carried all their necessities in the carro de caballos and slept in it at night. Roman was forced to leave his wife and continue sheepherding because he could not find any other employment. Roman Jaramillo had become an expert at his trade.

Roman left for the llanos, where the mountains end and the plains begin, near the Sierra de los Ladrones in Socorro. He was sure to take long ropes called *cabrestos*, which he placed around the ground on which he slept. The snakes would not go beyond the cabrestos, but if one happened to cross the large ropes, it would be seriously affected with the fumes of the *punche*, a type of tobacco placed under the bedding. Farmers planted the punche and then dried the large leaves, which were then ground and carried in small bags. Some people smoked it, but Roman never smoked the punche. Instead, he carried a little of it in the bottom of his mouth, between his teeth and lip. The sheep would be butchered, and then the hide would be hung out to dry. The hide canvas was large enough to completely cover the sheepherder's body, thus protecting him from the cold and especially the rain, which could not penetrate the wool hide. Any other bedding the sheepherder carried with him was rolled up within the hide and placed on a donkey to be carried to the next campground. Roman always had three donkeys with him. The large canisters of water used for drinking and cooking were tied with ropes and placed over the donkeys' backs. Roman's donkeys knew him, and he talked to them constantly. Once they were ready to move on, he would say to his lead donkey, "*Bueno ya vamos Precupio, ya estamos listos, ándale vamos.*" The burro would begin to walk, and the others would follow.

Roman would begin his journey to find at least five acres of grassland for the sheep and a watering hole. The sheep stayed together; they didn't wander off. He also had at least two or three trained dogs, which helped the sheepherder guide the sheep in the direction he wanted them to go.

Sometimes he traveled for hours before finding water. Roman would have to go into the mountain regions, where the dangers were much greater. Sheepherders didn't use their horses because horses could be spooked by snakes and other creatures in the llano, causing them to take off running. Their donkeys never ran away. They were more dependable, could carry more weight and, if the need arose, would last longer without food or water. Besides, this type of life was much too hard on their horses. They did not like using their horses this way.

Once Roman found water and settled the sheep in one place, he would take one of the sheep and walk it over to the water. The other sheep would follow. Eventually, the *caporales* would arrive at his camp to replenish supplies. The caporales would also report to the sheep owners about where the sheepherder had taken the sheep. During times of drought, they would report how many sheep were lost and any other news they felt was important for the owner to know.

On one occasion, Roman and another sheepherder, Marcimiliano Vallejos, ran out of punche. They had been hired by Abelino Aragón to take two separate partidas toward the Manzano Mountains. Abelino had become quite wealthy. He was married to María Vallejos, the eldest sister of Roman's mother, Felicitas. It was a good year. There were plenty of grasslands due to the amount of rainfall the year before, and the llano near the Ojuelos, an area filled with springs and ponds in the desert, had plenty of water for the sheep. Roman and Marcimiliano were only fifteen miles away from a supply store in Tomé. They left their mules and dogs in charge of the sheep one night and walked to Tomé to buy punche. They returned to their sheep before morning and found the caporal, Enrique Calles, waiting for them. "Where were you, and why were the sheep left alone?" Enrique inquired. Roman informed him that they had run out of punche and had waited two days for him to arrive with supplies. Enrique told them that they had problems with a herd led by sheepherder Beltrán Vallejos. A few days' earlier Beltrán's sheep had been attacked by several mountain lions. Beltrán and Enrique shot them, but they still lost several of the sheep. "What if this had happened here while you were gone?" Enrique questioned. "It didn't happen, and the sheep were under good care. My burros and dogs would have taken care of them. They are well trained. We bought the punche and returned immediately," replied Roman. Enrique told them he would not report them this time but ended with a strong warning: "Don't let it occur again!" That day, they cooked beans and made biscuits. Roman had become a very good cook. Included in the supplies Enrique had brought was dried

"*La Pastura* (The Pasture)," photograph by Ramón Juan Carlos de Aragón, 2010. © *Ramón Juan Carlos de Aragón*.

chile verde, green chile, which they also cooked with the carne seca they still had left from the last sheep they had butchered. They would have fresh meat for a couple days, but the rest was put up to dry for jerky. Enrique later married Roman's mother, Felicitas, who had been a widow for a few years.

Finally, Roman had completed his season of sheepherding, and winter was approaching. He would soon be able to return to his wife, whom he loved very much. They wanted a family, but after four years of marriage, they still had no children. Before heading for home, it was customary to butcher a lamb for fresh meat to take home to one's family. Roman would also take wool, which Candelaria used to make *colchones*, bedding, and beautiful embroidered wool-stuffed pillows. The three months home with his wife and family went by too fast. It was time to go back to work. This time, Roman found it especially hard to return to his sheep because Candelaria was finally expecting a child. He promised her this was his last sheepherding season. He heard that the WPA would soon be providing construction jobs for many of the people of the area. He wanted to be home with his wife to raise their child. He told Abelino Vallejos that he would not stay longer than three months because he wanted to be home for the birth of their child.

While the past year had been a good one for grass pastures and water in the Ojuelos, Roman and Marcimiliano found that the water was almost gone, and there was very little green grass for their sheep. They would have to part and travel in different directions to find food and water for their sheep. Roman took his partida and headed closer to the mountains, making sure that his rifle was always close by. One day, he passed by an Indian village out in the llano. The Indians invited him to join them to eat, and he graciously accepted. They told him of a water hole, which would probably be large enough for his sheep, about twenty miles away. He followed their directions, which led him farther into the mountains. There was a water hole and some grass, but it would not be enough to sustain his sheep for very long. On his first night there, a bear wandered into the camp. Roman stayed very still, and the bear soon walked away. He was glad he did not have to shoot the bear. Early the next day, he set out on his journey again. He walked and walked, and his burros, dogs and sheep followed along. For two days he walked and camped at night. The caporal never came, and his drinking water was gone. He was lost because he had never been to this area before. He had no idea where he could find water. That night, as he sat near the campfire, he realized this time he would not be returning home. He cried for his wife and unborn child, whom he would probably never see.

He was kneeling and praying to God, whom he called Tata Dios, when a stranger walked into the camp. The stranger called out his name, "Roman." "You are welcomed to eat some food, but I am sorry I have no water to offer," replied Roman. "I have not come to eat. I have come for you," replied the stranger. Roman asked him to come into the light of the campfire so that he could see him. It was impolite to speak to someone and not be able to see into his or her eyes. The dark figure approached, and Roman saw a skull. A long black cape covered the person's body and head. "Dios mío, eres la muerte, la Doña Sebastiana?" (My God, are you the Angel of Death?) cried out Roman. "But why have you come for me? I'm young, and my poor wife is with child. I'm sorry, but I won't go!" Roman proclaimed.

"What? You have no say in this," said Doña Sebastiana. "It is your turn. You will not find water in this deserted llano. Just give up. Why put yourself through any more of this misery? Now come with me!"

"But what will happen to my burros, my dogs and my sheep?" said Roman. "No, I will not go with you. I'm responsible for them, and I will not leave them."

"Come, I will not argue with you any longer," replied Death.

"Give me one more day," pleaded Roman. "Let me try to find them water. If I don't, you can take me tomorrow night. I will go with you then."

La Muerte Llama (Death Calls), print from *La Doctrina Cristiana* (La Revista Católica Publishing Co., Las Vegas, New Mexico), 1899. *Courtesy of the author.*

"Well, I have never done this before. You are a stubborn man. Very well, I will let you have another day. But I know there is no chance you will find water," said La Muerte. "I will be back tomorrow night, but you better be ready to come with me."

Roman felt weak and tired as he lay near the fire. Again he heard footsteps. "You said you would give me until tomorrow night. Why have you come back?" questioned Roman. He looked at the man who sat down near him, and suddenly he felt stronger. Roman sat up. He told the man, "I can offer you some food, but I have no water." The man took a biscuit and broke it, giving half to Roman and eating the other half. "Eat," he told Roman. Then the stranger said, "Look in that direction—what do you see?" Roman looked and saw balls of light moving up and down over the area. The stranger told him, "Go there in the morning." Then he was suddenly gone.

"*La Cienega* (The Spring)," photograph by Ramón Juan Carlos de Aragón, 2010. © *Ramón Juan Carlos de Aragón*.

As soon as there was enough light to see the next morning, Roman prepared his donkey, and he and his sheep and dogs followed their pastor. Roman was weak, but he walked for about seven miles toward where he had seen the lights, and there he found a treasure. There, in the middle of nowhere in the llano, was a small water hole. He walked one of his sheep to the water, and all the others followed. There was also enough grass for his sheep and donkeys to eat. To one end of the water hole were rocks piled up high, and dripping down from the rocks were pure, clear drops of water. He lay there below the rocks all day as the drops of water quenched his thirst.

As darkness came, so did La Sebastiana. She didn't want to show her shock at the renewed energy that Roman displayed. He was still weak from hunger, but he had saved part of his last biscuit and a few pieces of the carne seca for the following day. Roman greeted Sebastiana and offered her a seat by the fire. "Death, you must get pretty cold. Why don't you have a seat and warm yourself for awhile," Roman said.

"No, there is no time for that. I have been very busy. During a drought, there are many people who die from lack of food and water. Are you ready to come with me?" asked La Muerte.

"No, I said I would go if I didn't find water, but I did!" said Roman.

"Well, it might have saved you for a few hours, but you still have a long way to go," explained the Angel of Death. "No one will find you out here to supply you with water, and your sheep have already stripped this ground of the little grass it had. Just save yourself the misery and come with me now. You can not last much longer without grass for your sheep and water."

"Give me one more day. If I do not find water tomorrow, I will go with you tomorrow night," Roman again pleaded.

"Very well. You are really stubborn," said Death.

Roman prayed that the stranger would come once again and lead him to water. He strained his eyes to look for balls of light he had seen the night before, but he didn't see any. He got on his knees and again pleaded to God to be able to see his beautiful wife and be there for the birth of their child. He grew weaker and once again began to cry and lose hope. He heard footsteps. The stranger from the night before sat near the fire. Roman reflected on the kind eyes of the man who sat near him. Roman said, "I've saved this half biscuit and a few pieces of jerky, but I would be more than happy to share this with you. I have no water to offer." The compassionate stranger took the bread and once again broke it in half. He gave half to Roman and ate the other half. The stranger stood up and walked away, and just as suddenly as he appeared, he was gone. Roman looked in the direction that the stranger walked, and in the distance he could see dancing flames of light.

The next morning, Roman led his sheep, burros and dogs toward the lights. After a few miles, he could hear the sound of water gushing from the earth. The earth was as green as could be, and desert flowers of all colors sprung up from the ground. He took one of his sheep, and the rest followed it to a large spring of water. His animals ate. Later in the afternoon, Roman was shocked to see a white horse in the distance. As it approached, he could see the caporal Don Enrique. "You are a very hard man to find," said Enrique. "Here are your supplies." They cooked beans and green chile with carne seca and enjoyed a cup of coffee made from the fresh, clear spring water. Don Enrique left.

Roman waited anxiously for evening to come. He was happy. His burros, dogs and sheep were happy. He waited for Doña Sebastiana to come for a visit. Just like before, the Angel of Death approached the camp. This time she could not hide her surprise as Roman stood and walked toward her with a smile. "Come, come with me and have a seat by the fire. Warm yourself! I know you must always be cold. Please have some coffee, beans and this fantastic green chile I made with carne seca. I have to say I'm a very good cook," Roman exclaimed.

"Well, well. I do have to tell you I have never met anyone like you. You win! Go home to your wife and see your beautiful little baby girl, who was born before her time but is very healthy. I waited, but she had no need for me. I shall leave you now, but someday I will come for you, and you will not trick me again," Death said and walked away.

Roman returned home and found work with the WPA and never returned to sheepherding again. He told everyone who would listen about the time he met whom he thought was God in the desert. He built a house for his family. After the years they had waited to have a child, Roman and Candelaria were blessed with four children, whom they cherished and raised with pride. Not far from where he lived in La Constancia on the Loma de la Cruz, the hill with a cross, he and many others saw balls of light bounce and move around the area. What treasure lies there?

About the Author

When Ray John de Aragón was a little boy, his family's favorite pastime was storytelling. He always enjoyed listening to the older members tell about ghosts they claimed they heard or saw. They also told of witches who had lived nearby and about haunted houses. If dishes rattled, if furniture mysteriously moved or if musical instruments began playing on their own, everyone knew some unexplainable supernatural force was behind it. The stories were scary but exciting, and the author admits he had trouble sleeping at night. Ray John went on to major in American studies in college as an adult, further exploring the Spanish traditions, heritage and culture of New Mexico. This included the folklore. The author's interest is in preserving the oral "ghost" history of the region and passing it on to future generations.

Visit us at
www.historypress.net

This title is also available as an e-book